A LITTLE BOOK

OF

CHEESE

BY

OSBERT BURDETT

Was not that a great Cheese, think
you, wherewith Zoroaster lived in
the Wilderness twenty years together
without any other Meat?

Health's Improvement . . . By the
ever Famous Thomas Muffett,
Doctor in Physick. London, 1655

British Library Cataloguing-in-Publication Data
A catalogue record for this book is available from the
British Library

A History of Cheese

Caseiculture is the craft of making cheese. It most probably originated from nomadic herdsmen who stored milk in vessels made from sheeps' and goats' stomachs. Because the stomach linings of sheep and goats contains a mix of lactic acid, wild bacteria as milk contaminants and rennet, the milk would ferment and coagulate. A product reminiscent of yogurt would have been produced, which, through gentle agitation and the separation of curds from whey would have resulted in the production of cheese; the cheese being essentially a concentration of the major milk protein, casein, and milk fat.

Cheese itself is a thoroughly ancient food, whose origins predate recorded history. There is no conclusive evidence indicating where cheese-making originated, either in Europe, Central Asia or the Middle East, but the practice had spread within Europe prior to Roman times and, according to Pliny the Elder, had become a sophisticated enterprise by the time the Roman Empire came into being. The earliest evidence of cheese-making in the archaeological record dates back to 5,500 BCE, in what is now Kujawy, Poland, where strainers with milk fats molecules have been found. Alabaster jars containing cheese, have also been found at Saqqara (present day Egypt) – dating from around 3000 BCE. They most probably consisted of fresh cheeses coagulated with acid or a combination of acid and heat.

The earliest cheeses were likely to have been quite sour and salty, similar in texture to rustic cottage cheese or feta (a crumbly, flavourful Greek cheese). Indeed, from the third century BCE there are records of imported cheese (to Egypt) from the Greek island of Chios, with a twenty-five percent import tax being charged. Ancient Greek mythology credited Aristaeus (a minor god of culture, also credited with discovering bee-keeping) with the invention of cheese. By Roman times, cheese was an everyday food and cheese-making a mature art. Columella's *De Re Rustica* (c. 65 CE) details a cheese-making process involving rennet coagulation, pressing of the curd, salting, and aging. Pliny's *Natural History* (77 CE) devotes a chapter to describing the diversity of cheeses enjoyed by Romans of the early Empire. He stated that the best cheeses came from the villages near Nîmes (southern France), but did not keep long and had to be eaten fresh. A Ligurian (present-day northern Italy) cheese was noted for being made mostly from sheep's milk, and some cheeses produced nearby were stated to weigh as much as a thousand pounds each.

As Romanized populations encountered unfamiliar newly settled neighbours, cheese-making in Europe diversified further, with various locales developing their own distinctive traditions and products. As long-distance trade lessened (with the collapse of the roman empire in 700 CE), only travellers would encounter unfamiliar cheeses. This further led to regional diversification among European cultures, and resulted in the vast array of cheeses we have today. Charlemagne's first encounter with a white cheese that had an edible rind forms one of the constructed anecdotes of Notker's (840 - 912) *Life of the Emperor*.

The British Cheese Board claims that Britain has approximately 700 distinct local cheeses; France and Italy have perhaps 400 each. (A French proverb holds there is a different French cheese for every day of the year, and Charles de Gaulle once asked 'how can you govern a country in which there are 246 kinds of cheese!?') Still, the advancement of the cheese art in Europe was slow during the centuries after Rome's fall. Many cheeses today were first recorded in the late Middle Ages or after – cheeses like Cheddar around 1500, Parmesan in 1597, Gouda in 1697, and Camembert in 1791. Despite its relative novelty, cheese was immensely fashionable, and featured in many popular sayings. In 1546 The Proverbs of John Heywood claimed 'the moon is made of a greene cheese.' (Greene may refer here not to the colour, as many now think, but to being new or un-aged.) Variations on this sentiment were long repeated and NASA exploited this myth for an April Fools' Day spoof announcement in 2006.

The first factory for the industrial production of cheese opened in Switzerland in 1815, but large-scale production first found real success in the United States. Credit usually goes to Jesse Williams, a dairy farmer from Rome, New York, who in 1851 started making cheese in an assembly-line fashion using the milk from neighbouring farms. Within decades, hundreds of such dairy associations existed. The 1860s saw the beginnings of mass-produced rennet, and by the turn of the century scientists were producing pure microbial cultures. Factory-made cheese overtook traditional cheese-making in the World War II era, and factories have been the source of most cheese in America and Europe ever since.

Until its modern spread along with European culture, cheese was nearly unheard of in east Asian cultures, in the pre-Columbian Americas, and only had limited use in sub-Mediterranean Africa. But with the spread, first of European imperialism, and later of Euro-American culture and food, cheese has gradually become known and increasingly popular worldwide, though still rarely considered a part of local ethnic cuisines outside Europe, the Middle East, the Indian subcontinent, and the Americas. As is evident from this brief introduction to cheese and cheese-making however, it is a branch of cuisine with a fascinating and ancient history. We hope that the reader enjoys this book on the subject, and is encouraged to try some cheese-making for themselves.

'There is nothing abstract about good Cheese.'

CONTENT

¶ *The Illustrations are by Pauline Baumann*

The righteous minds of innkeepers
Induce them, now and then,
To crack a bottle with a friend
Or treat unmoneyed men;
But who hath seen the Grocer
Treat housemaids to his teas
Or crack a bottle of fish-sauce,
Or stand a man a Cheese?

From *The Flying Inn*
by G. K. CHESTERTON

TO RETURN THANKS

Writers are the slaves of circumstance and time, and this slavery has prevented me from making a cheese-tour of the English counties, without which even so modest an essay as this is temerarious. But, if we are fated to dwell in the House of Admetus, all the more grateful must we be to the friendly hands that come to us in our servitude, bringing gifts of information and help.

Particularly would I mention Mr Ernest Oldmeadow, an essayist of cheese; Mr John B. Firth, whose volumes in the 'Highways and Byways' Series cover the central (cheese) counties of England; both of whom supplied valuable references; the generous personal kindness of Miss Helen Simpson, whose The Cold Table *is only the latest evidence of her gastronomic erudition and experience; Mr J. B. Morton, for several useful tips; Messrs Cadbury Pratt, for much time and information freely placed at my disposal; also the London Library, the resource of all its members; and Mr Richmond Temple, of the Savoy, who spared no trouble to oblige his questioner. A Letter from Italy was a present indeed.*

The remarkable passage from the late Sir Rider Haggard's Rural England, *to be found in Chapter Three, is included by the kind permission of his Executors and of Messrs Longmans,*

'If there were nothing sacred and profound in Cheese, it would not have inspired so many jests.'

INTRODUCTION

'A book devoted exclusively to the appreciation of cheese has long been needed.' So wrote Mr Morton Shand eight years ago,[1] and so far as can be discovered such a book has yet to be written. But in the interval such clubs as the Saintsbury, which dines twice a year in honour of the great scholar and epicure whose name it bears, and the Wine and Food Society have arisen, to prove that bestial indifference to the arts of the table is being countered by the few, and that many people are combining to recover the guidance of a great tradition in the choice of what they drink and eat. The simple hope of the following pages, therefore, is to aid the reader in the choice of Cheese; to discuss the chief varieties available to him in England; to mention where some less common cheeses may be had; and not to bore or confuse him with technical details, fit indeed for cheese-makers and students for agricultural degrees but scarcely necessary at all to the enjoyment of a consumer.

Indeed, the expert or epicure of cheese is only considered here in so far as he may be provoked to break his silence. The writer is no more than an ordinary lover of cheese who, finding no elementary

[1] *A Book of Food,* by P. Morton Shand. Cape, 1927.

guide to help him in appreciation, has ventured to share with others in the like case such knowledge as he could come by fairly easily.

The variety that awaits us is scarcely realised, and many have hardly tasted more kinds of cheese than could be numbered on the fingers. Yet five hundred are mentioned in the books, and, if we exclude the fancy brands that are not true varieties, at least a hundred and fifty will remain. Indeed, not long ago the window of a London shop, in the endeavour to present a record number, was able to boast a display of two hundred different kinds.

Now, sharing the dismay that the ordinary reader will feel at such unheeded possibilities, and believing that we should begin at the beginning, the writer hopes to do no more than to discuss, say, half a hundred; for the cheese-eater who has gone no further will feel not only greatly enriched by his experience but will have arrived at the stage when he will prefer to add to his discoveries himself.

Discrimination must begin with the simple and the neglected, and there is little discrimination in England in the varied charms of cheese. Here, Cheese is a staple or a joke. In France it inspires public celebrations, and even statuary!

A few years ago there was unveiled at Camembert a statue to Madame Harel, the immortal inventor of the cheese that has made the name of its place of origin famous all over the world. If it be long before we reach a similar pitch of gratitude for our own triumphs, should we not blush to be unaware that Stilton is attributed to the genius of an Englishwoman, Mrs Paulet, of Wymondham in Leicestershire, and that it took its name from the Huntingdon village where her brother sold it at his inn, the Bell?

That we are content to be ignorant of such matters proves the subject of Cheese to be neglected, for they belong, as is shown in the great and allied literature of wine, to the appreciation of Cheese. This appreciation should have produced its literature, but when we begin to inquire we find plenty of technical handbooks for dairymen concerning the methods of manufacture, but for the consumer there is no more than a page or two. In the works of epicures or in casual essays by devotees of Cheese laments occur for the absence of something that they could, but have not yet, supplied.

The following pages are elementary; but, assured that the need they confess is increasingly shared, I offer them modestly, in the hope that they will be useful to the simple and may incite the learned to treat a profound and fascinating subject with the thoroughness that it has long deserved.

In my own preferences I have spoken frankly, for in matters of taste to be undogmatic is to be dull; but my wish is very far from dictating to others, the more in that, as with other underrated subjects, those who really

care for cheese, being few, are tempted to become
fanatical. Let that not be true of ourselves!

If the reader will allow for a devotee of green
among the firmer cheeses, and for the more savoury
and distinct flavours among the creamier, he will only
be aware of idiosyncrasies that may incite him to
assert his own.

CHAPTER ONE

OF CHEESE IN GENERAL

One of the oldest, simplest, and most nourishing of foods, Cheese differs from other staple forms of nourishment in that all but its softest kinds are equally good for a whole meal, and that all serve for a final benediction to it. As if this were not enough to proclaim its virtue, Cheese has the further distinction of mating equally well with wine or with beer—with that which is the glory of drinks and that which is the finest of thirst-quenchers. The meat-eater and the vegetarian are at one in its praises, and to the latter it takes with eggs the place of meat. Thus the solid food of the simple or the meatless diner has been called the 'wine-drinker's biscuit'—so well does its astringent flavour set off the subtle delights of wine and create with each mouthful a new zest for sipping. Cheese can also make a rare sandwich. There is, in truth, no service for the appetite that Cheese cannot fulfil: the hungry man, the poor man, the hasty traveller and the epicure have severally found it their blessing.

What, then, is this product of the dairy, and how does it come to be what it is? Cheese is the curd of milk which has been coagulated by rennet, separated from the whey, and then (as a rule) pressed. Its original advantage was that it turned one of the most perishable of foods, milk, into a solid that could be kept, and eaten over a long period. The many modifications possible to the process, not to mention the different kinds of milk and the different degrees of fat in the same kind, explain its many varieties. As with wine, each cheese originally took its name from the place of its origin; and it is the misfortune of England not to have copied the French practice and protected by law the original product. This can scarcely ever be exactly copied away from its home. The consequence is that our local cheeses are disappearing, and some, like the Banbury, often mentioned by Shakespeare, now exist only as names.

The usual classification of Cheese is threefold: into hard, semi-hard, and soft varieties. Many people, however, think of it merely by colour, and are only consciously aware of the yellow, the red, and the green or blue. With local names now implying nothing preciser than a type, and with factories turning out more or less standard types, and these in very different and absolutely undefined qualities, people consider themselves to be ranging afield when they seek one of those cheeses still identified, more or less, with a particular place or country. Broadly speaking, the hard cheeses are best for a meal, the soft for a sweet or dessert, and the semi-hard, which include the green cheeses, for eating with wine at the end of dinner. This, like other matters of taste, will be disputed, and some even aver that the best place for cheese is where it is least often found, that is to say at the very beginning, as it were an *hors-d'œuvre* to a meal. But *hors-d'œuvre* is not French for Unemployment.

With what should cheese be eaten? Actually, for the hard and semi-hard cheeses, there is nothing better than plain bread, if we would savour our cheese and not use it to fill up an odd corner at the end of dinner. For these cheeses bread is better than biscuit, for the ideal accompaniment of biscuit is simply butter. With the creamiest kinds, however, most of which are mild, biscuits are preferable. The softness of the soft cheese invites its complement—the crispness of biscuit—but it will be found that the flavour of crust, especially the adorable flavour of crust browned to the verge of blackness, is too strong for them. This also rules out damp, white, soft, or usual toast.

It is an old question whether butter should be eaten with cheese. Not, surely, with the creamier, nor with the most pungent; and, unless we wish to indulge in the superfluously rich, butter is a superfluity with green cheese. With other cheeses it is a matter of choice, the inherent indication being that the drier cheeses, some would say Gruyère and (to my mind) generally Cheshire, are enhanced by butter. Old nurses used to enforce bread and butter before their charges were allowed to add jam; and it may be that it was not only parsimony that dictated the adage, which the French carefully endorse, that cheese should be eaten without butter. Whatever the source, the adage exists, and traditions should be examined respectfully. They are the wisdom that has survived. Let us respect the adage as a Principle of Reference, but act according to our whim. Here, as elsewhere, the real mistake is to be fanatical about either.

The most difficult thing about common or popular cheese is to buy what you pay for: to find the genuine article under the name it bears, and to receive it in the condition without which you would not choose it. Whether in hotels, restaurants, or shops, few cheeses are protected from substitutes; and who has not suffered from Camemberts that are chalky instead of oozing, from Brie that has staled to a condition of yellow dryness, from a solid Port Salut, an india-rubber-like Bel Paese?

True Cheddar is the least discoverable of all, since the paradoxical effect of the factory and its standard-isation has been to flood the counter with such a number of concealed grades that the original cheese has almost disappeared under a swarm of inferior semblances. The only rule is to go where the best are professed to be sold, and there too to be prepared for disappointments. What the tradesman calls the West End taste has a standard of its own, of which a few (men's) clubs are the last stronghold. The less exclusive shops, especially beyond the West End, cater mainly for the less particular, who hate fine cheese, even though the variation in prices is not very great. There are ten tastes and therefore ten markets for cheese; and in the end the factory system makes a quick turnover paramount. Thus it is that the quickly made and the unmatured monopolise the grosser grocers.

On the other hand, the big shops generally supply some cheeses of excellent quality, and among them the inquisitive may find sometimes one or more of the local cheeses that often cannot be found in the towns nearest to their proper homes. The absence of complaint in regard to the haphazard quality of the common English cheeses is probably due to the destruction of taste by the only available and cheaper product: not to an original preference for insipid substitutes. Destroy the memory of a good thing, and in time its imitation under the old name will be *preferred* by most people.

This has happened to Cheddar, the most abused name in the world.

At this the epicure will leave it; but though, from his point of view, he is right, righteous indignation ignores something. If there ever was, there has long ceased to be a uniform flavour for Cheddar. Does it not cover the facts, while protecting a cherished

B

singularity, to admit that by this time Cheddar has become a word no more precisely descriptive than Sherry? As diverse flavours are now required of Cheddar cheese, and to some extent even of inimitable cheeses such as Stilton, as of the Jerez wines. Unfortunately, the differences are unreflected in nomenclature. Even the grocer's loose division of sherry into pale, golden, and brown, not to mention the individual names of the sherries included under each division, have no counterpart at a cheese-counter.

The epicure means the old, mellow, rich cheese that has been stored *after* ripening for a year, and to get it he must go, as a rule, to the traditional shops that scarcely offer any other. But even the young and mild cheeses have no true grading. The boasted uniformity of the factories achieves nothing more distinctively Cheddar than can be expected when a purchaser inquires after 'soap'. Buyer and seller must understand one another, and do in fact gravitate to counters where the same meaning is attached to the vaguest of English words.

CHAPTER TWO

ENGLISH CHEESES—FROM HARD TO SOFT

There are several reasons why the cheeses sold under the name of CHEDDAR are of such various quality that it is a complete toss-up what the purchaser receives. Real Cheddar was first made in Somerset, and the local process, the authorities tell us, was in use at least three hundred years ago. The cheese was made from two milkings: the evening's being added to the morning's milk. It was also kept and allowed to mature for the best part of a year. Nowadays much of that which passes for Cheddar is wanting in fat, and is kept for the shortest possible period before being marketed. It is made to be sold, not eaten.

A man who keeps his eye upon the counters of the grocers can sometimes make the comparison for himself. On these counters of nondescript cheddar there will, from time to time, appear a cheese marked 'Cheddar—Old English'. By comparison with these fakes, the old is found to be a ripe, richly flavoured and mellow cheese. The Old English has probably been kept for over six months, and has thus become the halfway cheese between those usually sold and those in the best shops which have probably been maturing for at least eleven. It is worth while for anyone habituated to a local grocer to seize this opportunity when it comes. Unless his palate has been acclimatised beyond recall to the insipid, it will respond with delight verging upon rapture to the true cheesiness of Cheddar.

There is never much of this Old English to be had, and the little that there is is snapped up by true cheese-lovers. Yet it is worth mention because it does appear in the ordinary multiple shops, and it is to the enforced frequenters of these that the slightest encouragement is welcome. The more insipid so-called Cheddars are poor in fat, have more water with the curd, and are cured more rapidly. So it is these which best suit the factories and the shops, equally insane on a quick turnover; and these, in their turn, have converted an acceptance of mild flavour into a demand for it, so that the imports from America include not only such types but the appetite that is content with them.

Since it requires an expert to judge a Cheddar by inspection of its rind, its texture, the absence of streaki-ness in its colour, and the way in which it should crumble between the fingers, the stock list of its visible qualities—including a smooth, hard, transparent rind—does not really help the purchaser. Unless or until qualities are graded, one must judge by experience and stumble in the dark. The test is the tasting. The flavour should be clean and full, with a pleasant but not a rasping bite, and with a suggestion of pepper, but neither hot nor acrid. If the cheese is pasty or leathery to the teeth, it is bad—for texture has taste when it is not indistinguishable from flavour. Cheese should be cheese, in the sense of being unmistakable; and English Cheddar, at its best, has a precision of savour that makes it, for Englishmen, the absolute 'norm' of the flavour characteristic of cheese. That is why no cheese-lover ever grows weary of Cheddar—if it be good.

Like butter, almost all our hard cheeses are—faintly or deeply—coloured, though most people are unaware of this until they come to CHESHIRE, which means, for them, the commonest English red cheese. This colour is caused by annatto, a substance prepared from the seed-pods of a plant found in South America and in the West Indies. Cheshire probably derives its high colour from a local preference, since the North of England prefers a deep tinge and the South a pale yellow.

But there is a white Cheshire which some prefer to the red, and as this white becomes veined with blue mould in its maturity, Blue Cheshire is a welcome alternative to those for whom Stilton or Wensleydale stands supreme. Blue Cheshire is usually to be found at its best in the dining-room of (men's) clubs. Ordinary red Cheshire is not so flaky as Cheddar but is granulated, and has a tendency to become very dry and almost dusty if not eaten in due time. It is a cheese encouraged to ripen early, which enables it to be put quickly on the market, and therefore it does not keep long. The white Cheshire, on the other hand, in order to become transfigured into blue, may require a period of eighteen months. It may be due to the slight difference in texture, but the flavour of red Cheshire seems (to me) flatter than that of Cheddar, as if the edge had been slightly blunted: a good cheese.

The chief cheeses whose county-names survive deserve a glance, though many cannot be found outside their own counties and though the fine shades of their differences can only be indicated summarily.

LANCASHIRE, whose local fame has unfortunately failed to penetrate to remoter districts of England, for it is almost unfindable elsewhere, is another cheese that ripens early and is not designed to keep. Its texture is looser. It is a cheese that can be spread with the knife, and at its best, when three months old, is mellow and delicious, with a clean and rich flavour. Any sign of acidity shows that it is under-ripe and indicates an age below the three months desirable.

Lancashire cheese boasts the further virtue that it is ideal for toasting. A ripe cheese, when toasted, has the consistency of a good custard and an unforgettably delicious taste. It is very crumbly and cohesive, some-what as icing-sugar is. Its richness of flavour is superb. It has the opulence of a fine old Madeira.

LEICESTER cheese claims to be the finest of all the mild hard cheeses of England. Like Lancashire, it is famous only in its own home, and is one of those cheeses which are rarely to be hoped for in London. A fine fellow, weighing forty pounds, it has the shape of a millstone, some eighteen inches in diameter and some four inches thick. Very bright in colour, and therefore very distinct, its texture is loose, flaky, and rather more crumbly than Cheshire itself. But any appearance of dryness should be deceptive, and it ought to leave a smear on the knife. The poor Leicesters are pasty and sweetish. The good are soft and flaky, and the flavour should be deliciously rich. Its period of ripening should be at least a couple of months, and (like cheeses of more leisurely growth) it keeps extremely well. The traveller may hope to find it in the chief towns of the Midlands.

DERBYSHIRE cheese, when good and when made in the original way, resembles Leicester, another millstone, but rather smaller in weight and in size. It is one of the oldest of English cheeses, the secrets of whose making were jealously kept, so that the product of the different dairies in the county varied considerably. A uniform Derbyshire was, happily, unknown. Now, as with other cheeses, its method has been the subject of research, but little cheese is now made in the county. Requiring the same time to mature as Leicester, Derbyshire also keeps well.

WILTSHIRE can be described most simply as a small Cheddar.

The county of Gloucester has given its name to two cheeses, SINGLE GLOUCESTER and DOUBLE GLOUCESTER, the latter being the better known.

Both seem to differ locally from the appearance and size familiar in London, when, indeed, Single Gloucester can be had there at all. Non-Gloucester folk know and admire Double Gloucester as the aristocrat of English red cheeses. In shape, it is the size of a large grindstone with convex edges—flat, round, and large. Its texture is close and crumbly: a glorified Cheshire cheese. It has a pronounced, but mellow, delicacy of flavour, being pungent without being sharp. The tiniest morsel is pregnant with savour, nor does an ordinary greedier mouthful disappoint or cloy the palate. To measure its refinement, it can undergo the same comparison as that we apply to vintage wines.

Begin with a small piece of red Cheshire. If you then pass to a morsel of Double Gloucester, you will find that the praises accorded to the latter have been no whit exaggerated. Though popularly regarded as something of a rarity in places distant from Berkeley, where it was originally made, it is usually to be had in good West End shops. A slow-ripening cheese, it keeps reasonably well, but in its early days it suffers from draughts, and when cut, however ripe, has the tendency of crumbly cheese to become dry and friable. To mature properly it needs, say, six months.

SINGLE GLOUCESTER, made during spring and summer, on the other hand, needs but a couple of months to mature. It is usually white, and is of a kindred shape, the same as Double, but smaller and flatter, and from this, though opinions differ, it presumably derives its name. Being a quick-ripening cheese, Single Gloucester has a texture not close but open, not firm but soft. Its mild flavour commends itself to its admirers, but it would be uncritical to compare its freshness with the mellow maturity of Double Gloucester. The quick-ripening and the slow-ripening cheeses are as different in quality of flavour as a young and crisp from an old vintage wine. Each offers distinct pleasures, which it would be a mistake to confuse. One suits one type of meal and weather, the other an opposite type of each.

Single Gloucester is good for toasting.

Another cheese from the West, less famous, but not hard to find in London, is CAERPHILLY. This Welsh cheese, now made widely beyond the Principality, is small, round, very white and fairly firm. In taste and texture it should be creamy, with a delicate, faint, pleasant bite. The more you eat of it the more tasty it is. Women respond delightedly to its blandness. It is important to eat Caerphilly, as indeed all quickly ripening cheeses, at the right moment. It matures in less than a fortnight, but does not usually keep for longer than three weeks. Though it belongs to the class of hard-pressed cheeses, the curd of Caerphilly is full of moisture and, consequently, must be eaten without loss of time. When past its best, it becomes dry, hard, and rather suggestive in texture of crumbly chalk. It is said to be one of the easiest of cheeses to make. Though best in early summer, it can be made all the year round, and it has the advantage of yielding as much as a pound and a quarter to a gallon of milk, and of producing a quick return because it needs so little storage. Outside London, Caerphilly can be obtained most readily in Somerset and round about Bristol, but, though it is now ubiquitous in the West, I recall a public and timely complaint by Mr Ernest Oldmeadow that he had been unable to find it in Cardiff, but a few miles from its original home.

STILTON, as has been mentioned, derives its name from the village in Huntingdonshire where, at the Bell Inn, it was first sold in the last decade of the eighteenth century by its inventor's (Mrs Paulet) kinsman, Cooper Thornhill. 'You used to see', wrote the Rev. T. E. Gretton in *Memory's Harkback* (1889), 'a great pile of them [Stiltons] in front of the house, and a smart traffic was done with the travellers and coach-passengers.'

Though its making spread first to Dalby, and since throughout Leicestershire and even in Nottinghamshire and Rutland, Stilton is happily still strongly entrenched in its native home and, so long as its quality is maintained, need fear no competition. It survived, a generation ago, a passing threat from Roquefort. It has no fear of Gorgonzola. The Dutch have tried, and failed, to imitate it. The original Stilton remains supreme. Its cylindrical shape and rough grey rind (which should not be too heavy) need no description, though emotion kindles at the familiar sight.

When choosing one, beware of cracks that show the cheese to have been kept in a draught; observe that the blue mould is evenly distributed all over its surface, and that its colour between the blue veins is that of a full cream. Whiteness betrays immaturity, a sharp taste, and poor quality. Gastronomically speaking, never less than half should be purchased at a time, for Stilton, the majesty of English cheese, is wasted on those who do not appreciate it royally. Even a household of two should have no difficulty in consuming a quarter, and we shall find that there is excuse for the practice of the highest class of cheesemonger which still, sometimes, forbids its purchase by the pound. Its best season is from November to April, though it is now offered for sale in the bad shops throughout the year; but, clearly, the majestic cheese, like the weightier wines, is most enjoyable when the appetite is keenest during autumn and winter, and when fullness of flavour and body give solidity as well as mellowness their amplest scope.

A diner's long experience of Stilton convinces me that, once the cut Stilton shows signs of dryness, no libations of port or old beer avail. All they do is to produce an unsightly appearance, and to convict the household resorting to them of neglect and high treason to the cheese. A method of postponing the inevitable evaporation caused by the exposure of the inner surface to the air will be mentioned in a moment. If the cheese is eaten with the zest and regularity that are second nature to its admirers, their appetite will make any substitute unnecessary. Its fate should be to disappear, never to dry.

Another lesson, learned with joy, was that the riper a promising Stilton is allowed to become the more it approaches the pluperfect. The story of this experience may be worth mention.

One autumn, in the very old and small-windowed grocery of a little county-town, we selected a whole cheese by the deliberate method of inserting a cheese-trier into several. (This removes a plug from the heart of a cheese which, once its inmost end, for tasting, has been taken from it, can be re-inserted, thus leaving the rind airtight again.) A month later we repeated the trial and, in spite of the grocer's assurance that the Stilton was perfectly mature, we waited a month, tried yet again, and in the end declined to accept the Stilton, which had been chosen in November, until the following February. The perfection of flavour then reached is unforgettable.

The Stilton, being a good one to begin with, had become as mellow as an aged and great wine. I shall never hope to surpass it. Here I must guard myself by explaining that I do not mean deliquescent or mite-y by this term. I mean a very blue, in places yellowing, and still moist or creamy cheese, with some brown patches indeed near its circumference, but everywhere mellow as a great Madeira and nowhere dry or such as could not be offered to a vegetarian. How good it was can be guessed from the truth that it remained enjoyable to the end, even though designed for a household of two persons with no more factitious aid than the appreciation of chance visitors and the real difficulty of procuring other solid food in those waning months of the War. We were able, and delighted, largely to live on it. It was finished, like a great bottle, with a sigh of gratitude and regret.

Normally, however, the small household, willing to experiment with half a Stilton, can, if they really appreciate the cheese, preserve a good one from dryness simply by the method in which it is cut. Ordinarily and with careless ease, one scoops it from the centre with a cheese-spoon or a knife. But, if one wishes to take special care at the table itself, it can be sliced in sections, not downward but horizontally. Obviously, a much smaller surface is exposed to the air by cutting its surface into sections from the centre. Each section, roughly triangular and not more than three-quarters of an inch thick, can be a helping of the size each person wishes, and, since all helpings are of the same depth, the surface remains almost as flat—and the same size—as when the cheese was first cut into halves. In fact, when each round is completed, the surface will, of course, be flat again, and again. In this way also the cheese can be closely covered with grease-paper in the larder because the paper can lie naturally upon or nearly upon the entire exposed surface of the cheese. When the cheese is scooped out, there is necessarily a much larger and awkwardly shaped surface exposed. This, being in the form of an irregular hole, cannot be protected from the air so closely. The precaution suggested is effective, but it is pleasanter to eat the cheese with a will and to scoop it out in the usual manner.

As is to be expected from its quality, Stilton is a slow-ripening cheese, requiring time, care, and leisure to attain its virtue. A horrid cheese, though blue-veined, can be produced in six weeks, but it looks white and anæmic, and is only to be mentioned by way of warning. The genuine Stilton requires from three to six months to ripen; and that, remember, means that only then is it fit *to appear in the shops*.

We have seen reason to know that such cheeses, in fact, appear at the earliest moment, and that *maturity* only begins when this technical 'ripeness' is past.

The producer, having to wait patiently for his Stilton to become marketable, will necessarily term it 'ripe' so soon as it is in a condition to be sold. *His* client is not the consumer but the middleman; and only the best of the latter can afford the time, and the storage, the cellar-room, to allow the 'ripe' cheese still further to develop its quality before it is offered for sale to a discriminating consumer. Labour costs!

There are reasons, then, why some of the better cheese-merchants still sometimes refuse to sell Stilton by the pound. Its worthy admirers will be almost as unwilling to risk its piecemeal dispersal to chance customers as a wine-merchant is to sell his bottled wines by the glass. There is, however, some demand for that which epicures would dismiss as white Stilton; and, of course, a young one can be hacked about with impunity by those who like it in its raw state. All this shows the various tastes that even good cheesemongers have to allow for. The risk and expense of making fine Stilton, recorded elsewhere in these pages, and the further expense of its storage once 'ripe', explain why a Stilton of the best quality is still sold, in some of the good shops, only by the whole or by the half.

Cheese-mites, it should be remembered, attack a cheese from the outside and bore their way toward the centre. Maturing Stiltons, therefore, have to be brushed daily and provide full-time employment for men whose chief occupation this is. Blessed labour!

BLUE CHESHIRE has already been mentioned as a pleasant alternative to Stilton, but it seems to me to lack majesty and to have a tendency to become dry. It is, however, extremely enjoyable, one of the traditional pleasures of a good (man's) club. The reasons why it is not easy to buy are that it is reserved for such regular customers, that the supply is small and irregular, that it is not properly a distinct cheese.

A cheeseman of forty years' experience told me that all Cheshire is red to begin with; but that an uncertain few, which have to be accepted rather than made, begin to show signs of pallor. This small percentage, eagerly marked for Clubs and special customers, will develop a blue mould if kept after they have lost their original carroty colour. Any Cheshire, he added, that is inclined to pale can be nursed by the cheeseman and, through heat and appropriate treatment, be helped upon its path. But not more than half a dozen in a hundred show signs of this vocation. He showed me one the outer parts of which were almost iridescent, with the effect of mother-of-pearl. It palely approached the lovely blend of tints, from black to pale pink, blue and yellow that were the favourite harmonies on the fans and silks of Charles Conder. This cheese was in the agony of conversion, a beautiful sight to the sympathetic eye.

We therefore pass to WENSLEYDALE, the superlative Yorkshire cheese, which is a rival to Stilton in the friendly sense that Bordeaux and Burgundy are sometimes said to be rivals.

Wensleydale, of the same shape, but slightly smaller than Stilton, should not have a smooth coat, for this betrays both a hard cheese and a harsh flavour. A good Wensleydale is more delicate than Stilton as, in a

C

sense, Claret is more delicate than Burgundy. The cheese should be creamy, rich, subtle in flavour, and be soft enough to spread, and its blue should branch uniformly over its surface. It would not be possible to savour Wensleydale after Stilton, but it could, perhaps, be eaten before; though one can understand its wise admirers asserting that it would be shameful to eat any other cheese, green or otherwise, after it. For delicacy, and many would add, for after-savour, the exquisite Wensleydale must receive the crown. As befits its quality, Wensleydale requires about six months to ripen. The chief difference in its making is that, unlike Stilton, Wensleydale is a pressed cheese. Its rare delicacy is becoming better known, and it is one of the few local English cheeses which, instead, alas, of dying, has spread its reputation beyond its own county in the past few decades.

COTHERSTONE is another Yorkshire cheese, which is compared with Wensleydale, and said to be moister, but I have never had the good fortune to try it.

A fifth blue cheese is DORSET, or 'Blue Vinny' (for veiny), still a local product, but said, occasionally, to be found in a few West End shops. If so, I have been unlucky. About the size of a Stilton, and with a rough rind, its texture is stiff and crumbly, and its veins should branch evenly throughout the curd. One reason why it is unlikely to spread is that its making offers a peculiar difficulty. In fact, local cheeses have died because the milk trade has become the most profitable form of dairywork—through the speed of modern transport, the saving of labour and expense, the quick turnover milk secures: all evil in their results.

All this suits our soulless combines and trusts. They buy up all the milk they can, and thereby displace local products with the standardised, and inferior, produce of their own factories.

Now, Blue Vinny happens to be made from skimmed milk. Consequently, its making involves the churning of butter as well as the making of cheese. Its makers are thus confronted with the competition of huge supplies of imported butter, and it may be said that there is every temptation to abandon the making of Blue Dorset except for local demand. It is prudent, then, to miss no chance of trying this cheese before the threat to its existence shall prove overwhelming, and charitable not to grumble at the high price that its best quality maintains. It is further at the mercy of uncontrolled conditions, because the milk is at the mercy of the atmosphere and temperature for a few hours before it is ready, after skimming, to be used. Again, the time required for the blue veins to grow varies with the kind of curd and with the season. The moister curds will ripen in a couple of months, but the harder may require six months, if not more.

Blue Vinny is compared—like all blue cheeses!—

with Stilton; but its reputation for a rather sharp
flavour suggests comparison with Gorgonzola.
It is for each reader to decide.

Leaving the hard, and the semi-hard, blue cheeses
behind us, we come to the soft or CREAM-CHEESES.
Here the variety, even apart from numerous proprietary
brands, makes detailed examination impossible.

To the amateur of the harder cheeses, English cream-
cheeses may appear to have a family likeness, a mutual
resemblance more pronounced than in their foreign
rivals; though this, doubtless, the esurient will deny.
Perchance the truth is that a palate for hard cheeses
and a palate for soft cheeses of the English variety are
different. Though by no means necessarily, as the
French soft cheeses conspicuously show, cream-cheeses
here are usually mild. New varieties, sometimes the
adventurous product of a single country dairy, not
infrequently appear and disappear in London, so that
cream-cheeses come and go like other fashions in the
market. They can also be fanciful. A very inviting-
looking one, for example, that I saw lately was made
sandwich-wise, with a layer of cream between each
layer of cream-cheese. It looked like a streaked brick
of liquefying ivory. Indeed, it is under the heading
of 'fancy cheeses' that the cream-cheeses are often
grouped in the shopmen's lists, so that only an arbitrary
selection can be attempted here.

At its simplest, cream-cheese almost makes itself. You pour your cream into 'a perforated box lined with loose muslin', wait for a few days, and in a week it should be dry or 'ripe'. So perishable a dainty, too, should remain a dairy-product and be eaten on the spot. It is not well designed for transport. As Mrs Beeton observed: 'Cream-cheese, although so called, is not properly cheese, but is nothing more than cream dried sufficiently to be cut with a knife'. Yet how much they differ!

Cream-cheeses, when not only dried cream, are generally made from sweet fresh milk, unripened by any acidity until after rennet has been added, are not pressed, are small and as soft as good butter. The difference is that the whey is never allowed to drain entirely from them. This moisture permits the fermentation to grow quickly, and the absence of heating and pressing furthers, of course, the same end. The ripening proceeds from the circumference to the centre. Consequently, the temptation is to place them on the market too soon, and when this has happened the purchaser finds a cheese oozy at its surface but sadly callous in the centre. Being short-lived, they are often salted or refrigerated for transport, so a genuinely creamy cream-cheese is found less by cunning than by grace.

Pride of name and of position must be given to SLIPCOTE, one of the oldest, which used to be considered the best of English cream-cheeses. Made in Rutland, and familiar until the War, it is apparently unobtainable in London. But, while it is no use to ask for Slipcote or Slipcoat in London, where the Past is beginning to be despised as well as destroyed, if you ask for YORK you may be given something like it. This brick-shaped, thin-rinded cheese, lying on its straw mat, bears out the description of Slipcoat. It was small, and when mature rather like a Camembert—which sets the norm for the subtler flavours of soft cheeses as Cheddar does for the hard, and Stilton for the semi-hard, varieties. Slipcote derived its name from the ease with which its coat or rind detached itself from the mellow ooziness within. In general, cream-cheese (other than dried cream) distinguishes itself by a faint and very pleasant savour of sourness, as if extremes had met—as they do in the beauty of grotesque, to be extreme, or in those moments of illumination when the poet sings of 'all the sadness in the sweet, the sweetness in the sad'. The essential virtue of such cream-cheese is the sweetness in the sour. 'Under the tree where thy mother was debauched, I have redeemed thee', so to speak.

But there are sweet cream-cheeses also. Take, for example, VICTORIA cream-cheese. This, the full-cream-cheese made at Guildford, and to be had at Messrs Cadbury Pratt in Bond Street, is a perfection of pure cream. It has the flavour of the freshest dairy-butter—butter that is *not* to be confused with the poor butter often offered under this description in towns—but raised, as it were, one degree beyond it. In texture it resembles cream-cheese, however. Like butter, it is made all the year round, and requires to be eaten without addition unless, perhaps, a pinch of salt. To those who have a palate for true butter, and who wish for a cheese with a butter flavour, Victoria can be recommended confidently.

GUILDFORD cream-cheese, virtually not so very distinguishable from Victoria, and made by Messrs Cow & Gate, at Guildford, is very good. Messrs Paxton & Whitfield, Jermyn Street, stock it.

The so-called NEW FOREST cream-cheese is really half a Victoria.

A convenient and agreeable brand of cream-cheese is HORNER'S cream-cheese, made at Redditch in Worcestershire. It is neither ambitious of surpassing the virtue of butter, nor is it at all too sour. It is much better than many newer brands, and may be called a good standby. No one could dislike it.

The little COTTSLOWE, a factory-made Cotswold cream cheese with a cheddar flavour, is not remarkable. Nor is the FARM VALE, sold in little boxes of eight and wrapped in silver paper, which is made at Wellington in Somerset. Many brands, sold as cream-cheeses, are really made of very raw Cheddar or Cheshire, unmatured and called 'cream'! Designed for flat-dwellers and to be put on the table without thought, some are fitter to sell than to swallow. Real cream-cheeses will not keep for long. In the cold weather they tend to brown and dry up: in the warm to become rancid. Theirs is the beauty of ephemeral things, and by this they are distinguished from their counterfeits. The refrigerator is a dangerous 'friend' for them.

ST IVEL, made at Yeovil, is a soft cream-cheese said to be rich in the 'sour milk' microbe, now less fashionable and gone the way of other scientific panaceas.

CORNISH cheese I have read of, but never tasted, a little cheese, as I am told.

Then there is CAMBRIDGE cream-cheese which, like others of the family, is a seasonal cheese for the summer. They weigh about a pound, should appear on the straw-mat used to drain them, and have roughly the shape of a brick. Whether the name means much is doubtful, for a similar cheese is sometimes called YORK. This Cambridge or York cheese used, I am told, to be a favourite before the War with Greeks and Russians, perchance reminding them in their exile of a similar native product. My informant implied that it needed a foreign palate and appeared soft and insipid to many Englishmen forgetful of Slipcoat.

It is sometimes said that neither Scotland nor Ireland has a native cheese, though this always sounds incredible of Ireland, the home of dairy-farming. Mr R. Hedger Wallace, however, mentions DUNLOP—'the only variety now known' in Scotland, and adds: 'According to a tombstone at Dunlop, these sweet milk cheeses were first made in the time of Charles II by Barbara Gilmour, who learnt how to make such cheeses in Ireland'.[1] Mr Belloc, in an essay, alludes in passing to Dunlop cheese, and says it is 'made in Ayrshire: they could tell you more about it in Kilmarnock'. It is said to be hard and like Cheddar, and a whole cheese to weight about fifty-six pounds. It won praise from Mrs Beeton, who observed: 'Dunlop has a peculiarly mild and rich taste; the best is made entirely from new milk'.

The statement that Ireland has no cheese is made so often, and is so hard to believe, that a demur from Mr J. B. Morton, of whom I inquired, is welcome. He referred to the Cheddar-like cheese of CONNEMARA as one of several local Irish cheeses. Perhaps, like other little local things, they will not travel, but are as worthy to be tried upon the spot as many a *vin du pays* is in France.

[1] *Notes and Queries,* Twelfth Series, Vol. IV, p. 190.

CHAPTER THREE

AN OLD RECIPE FOR STILTON

The making of cheese, once a craft, has become a trade since research has analysed, in part, the process that was originally experience by rule of thumb. For the appreciation of cheese a knowledge of its making is scarcely necessary, and the little that need be said here has therefore been interpolated to give a glimpse and no more of the process, a highly technical and various one.

The period from May to September is the natural season for cheese-making because the milk should then be at its best. Upon the quality and the amount of the fat in the milk the quality of most pressed cheeses depends. Often the milk used is a blend of the morning's with the previous evening's milk: some old-fashioned people say because one is always richer in fat than the other, and others merely because the evening's milk has had time to begin to ripen, that is to sour, especially if it has been kept at a temperature to encourage acidity.

This was the old rule of thumb method.

The modern scientific one is to use a 'starter', that is to say, a preparation of lactic acid bacteria obtained from agricultural institutes. The amount to be added varies with the kind of cheese to be made. Next the milk is heated, and then, if any, the colour is added: formerly a preparation from the juice of marigolds or carrots. The milk is now ready to receive the rennet— a soluble ferment found in the stomachs of calves and other young mammals—and it is the action of the rennet that produces the curd which, when strained from the whey, will become by various treatments the kind of cheese desired. The heating of the curd is called 'cooking'. Salting follows, after which the curd is placed in the moulds which will give the cheese its shape. Then pressing, turning, storing complete the process until the cheese is ready for the market where, as we have seen, it may still need to be matured, by keeping, from anything up to a year or even eighteen months.

Some cheeses, for example Cheshire, are made in three kinds: early, medium, and slow ripening. The early are mild, the medium mellow, the slow richest in flavour. The former suit the factories and the multiple shops, equally intent on a quick turnover. The latter suit those who can afford to wait, and who appreciate the leisurely and exquisite reward of waiting.

It is said that cheese must be made either by small-holders or in factories, because constant personal oversight can be ensured only at either extreme of organisation. It is to ensure uniformity of product that the textbooks of cheese-making are written, but for the enjoyment of the reader a record of the old rule of thumb method is better: uniformity is soulless.

Such I chanced to find in the late Rider Haggard's exhaustive survey, *Rural England*. This was written thirty years ago and contains the account he received from the lips of Mrs Musson, of Wartnaby, who was locally famous for her Stiltons.

Mrs Musson wins our hearts by remarking that Stiltons, 'with the exception that they make no noise, are more trouble than babies'. The process that she used in rearing them she described to Rider Haggard as follows:

'First, the milk that came from Shorthorn cows—which she considered the best for the purpose, although some makers keep other breeds of cattle—was strained or sieved into a big tin vat, where it stood until it had cooled down to 80 degrees. At this temperature the rennet is put in, which coagulates the milk and turns it into curd. As to the amount of rennet necessary to this end there seems to be no fixed rule—at least in this matter Mrs Musson said she was guided by experience.

When the curd is ready it is ladled out with a big scoop into straining-cloths, which are placed over a curd-sink, the whey, which is used for pig-food, running into a cistern outside the chamber. Here the curd remains to ripen in the surplus whey for a length of time which depends on the weather and other conditions. When the weather is hot it would, I was informed, mature in about forty-eight hours, the cloths meanwhile being tightened from time to time.

'After this the curd was broken up and, salt having been added to the amount of 7 lbs. or 8 lbs. to 25 lbs. of curd, the whole is put into a hoop with holes in it, but neither top nor bottom, through which the whey drains. In these it stands for seven or eight days, the whole mass being turned each day. Occasionally, also, skewers are driven into the hoops to assist in ridding them of the whey.

'On the seventh or eighth day it is slipped out of the hoop and invested with a binder or cloth, which is changed every day for another eight days or so, the cheese being turned at the same time. When the binder cloths are found to be quite dry upon the cheese, the use of them is discontinued. By this time the cheese should have assumed that wrinkled appearance with which we are familiar in Stilton.

'It is then moved into a coating room (which must be kept damp and have a cool draught of air passing through it, where, Mrs Musson said, it remains for a week or more) and the surface assumes its light grey colour. After this it is transferred to the storeroom, that should be damp and dark, where it is turned and brushed daily for a period of about six months, during which time it sinks from 18 lbs. to 14 lbs. or 15 lbs. in weight. [Damp and dark is right for wine-cellars.]

'Now, if all things have gone right, it should be a perfect Stilton cheese and ready for eating. . . . So far as I could discover, it takes about five quarts of milk to make 1 lb. of curd, and 25 lbs. of curd to make a ripe Stilton of 15 lbs. weight. Mrs Musson continued to make cheeses up to the end of November, but when the frost came the curd began to go back in quality. . . . It should be added that the excellence of the cheese depends greatly on the quality of the grass on which the cows are fed.'[1]

The descriptions given in the textbooks sound much more technical than this, and naturally such agreeable phrases as 'no fixed rule' or 'when the curd is ready' are very carefully desiccated in them.

Nevertheless, we are grateful to Sir Rider Haggard for having preserved this conversation with Mrs Musson who, as a proficient disciple of the old, unscientific, and successful method, deserves to be remembered in company with Mrs Paulet, of Wymondham, who had invented Stilton cheese more than a century before. The twenty villages in Belvoir Vale are the historic centre of the Leicestershire cheese

[1] *Rural England,* by Sir H. Rider Haggard. 2 vols., Longmans, 1906.

industry, and long may the fame of its makers, at any rate, continue to 'make a noise' in the world. The great English cheeses are still insular glories. Only what the French call Chester seems to be known in Europe, though a quarter of a century ago Stilton had, I believe, a small but regular market in Germany.

The Cheddar process, by the way, is known to have been used in Somerset for nearly three hundred years. In 1950, let us hope, enough of the original Cheddar will continue to be made to justify tercentenary celebrations in Somerset; but if our dwindling number of surviving English cheeses is to be preserved, cheese-eaters must become more vocal and collective in their appreciation. We few, we fit if few, must choose, and praise, and pray.

This summer one correspondent in *The Times,* where letters on the subject of ices had been appearing, invited that newspaper to make us more 'cheese-conscious'. We may take him to represent a number who do not write letters to newspapers but who none the less desire the better, wider, and more discriminating appreciation of English cheese.

On this depends the survival of the unextinguished English cheeses.

CHAPTER FOUR

A CHOICE OF FOREIGN CHEESES

The emphasis on English, at the end of the previous chapter, was made in no exclusive spirit. Only, the cheeses that are in danger of disappearing are primarily our English ones.

It needs nothing more adventurous than a trip to the market at Calais to discover a variety of cheeses that we have largely lost at home. This is only one instance of English indifference, the price we pay for industrialism in one of its thousand wicked forms.

We discard or throw away or accuse of unpalatableness, and even of poison, many kinds of food that are prized, made tasty by good cooking, and found perfectly safe to eat in France. Her fish-markets abound in pike, perch, and other fresh-water fish equally common in English rivers, fish that our anglers enjoy to catch but scarcely think of eating, fish that, if brought home, nobody in England knows how to cook. All but one of our edible fungi are considered poisonous, whereas the dangerous toadstools are easily recognisable and few—as can be learned, even without the personal guidance of an enthusiast, from the pamphlet published by the Ministry of Agriculture on *Edible Fungi*, with its useful coloured illustrations.

Perhaps it was this French prudence, and catholicity of taste, that made Brillat-Savarin confine his discussion of cheese to one of the great Aphorisms that introduce the *Physiologie du Goût:*

'Dessert without Cheese is like a pretty woman with only one eye.'

In Soho, and in Archer and Charlotte Streets, a fair variety of foreign cheeses can be seen, bought and tasted. Our concern, moreover, is with the foreign cheeses that are available *here.* We shall follow the same division that we used in regard to the cheeses of England, and proceed from hard to soft rather than from country to country.

The 'happy country where huge cheeses grow', celebrated by Gray in one of his *Letters,* was Parma, and PARMESAN is, of course, the hardest cheese in the world. Stone dead hath no fellow, nor has a Parmesan cheese. With the smallest percentage of moisture, it is naturally the longest lived, and Mrs Beeton said that such (the skimmed milk) varieties were 'made for sea-voyages principally'. The hardest Parmesan needs two or even three years to mature, and when choosing it the first thing to look for is a surface generously and evenly mottled with white spots. It is so hard that no cheese-trier is used to test it, but it is judged by a hammer, as a wall is judged by the sound of taps and blows.

Parmesan and Grana, its kindred, are made from
D

cow's milk partly skimmed, and the first advantage of its hardness and absence of moisture is its resistance to heat in a warm climate, and to time. As everyone knows, its chief use is for enhancing the flavour of soups, sauces, macaroni, and spaghetti, for which it must be grated into a powder. Indeed, its flavour appears to be brought out by pulverising, and, as it were, to be released by the ingredients with which it is mixed. Tried alone, as an experiment, in thin veils, Parmesan falls short of its quality in another vehicle. It fulfils its finest function for the wine-drinker when served as a savoury in the form of cheese-straws.

For eating, of course, the younger and less hard Parmesan is used, and can be very agreeable. 'It is the world', says Mr Belloc finely, 'that hardens Parmesan. In its youth the Parmesan is very soft and easy, and is voraciously devoured.'

The English jokes made about cheese usually fix upon GORGONZOLA, the stock green cheese of the English people, and this is remarkable since it long maintained the boast of being made in Italy alone. Its imitations seem to have begun in Denmark fifty years ago. They have been tried elsewhere, but the original Italian cheese is still so widely exported that no one who looks at what he is buying need be fobbed off with a substitute.

Gorgonzola is the name of a village, now almost a suburb of Milan, whence it can be reached by tram. The cheese is made throughout this neighbourhood, and, being a semi-hard cheese and therefore obsequious to heat, has to be carried to the cooler Alpine valleys for its ripening. Even so, Gorgonzola is subject to attack by moulds on its surface, a surface normally showing a tendency to slime. Therefore this cheese is as variable in quality as Cheddar. The green mould within is encouraged by the holes punched in the cheese, and the veins leading to them betray the course of the puncher. Consequently, it is truer to say that the moulds need air-space in order to grow than that the cheese is 'artificially ripened' by copper wire or the like. None the less, that the mould, which is techni- cally the same as that in Roquefort, needs air seems to account for the difference in flavour between Gorgon- zola and those green cheeses which ripen without such punctures. Backward Stiltons, by the way, are some- times ripened by the insertion of moulds from older cheeses. There are endless tricks in the trade.

Though excellent, the flavour of Gorgonzola is sharp and, by comparison, cruder than that of an English blue cheese, just as its substance is whiter, and more elastic than buttery. Since it does not keep long, we must not ask of it the mellowness, the subtlety of savour, the lingering caress, that the cheeses capable of age reserve for connoisseurs. You either like Gorgonzola or you dislike it. It is to 'vintage' cheeses as a good *vin ordinaire* is to vintage wines, and though some of these last can be excellent value for their money, and are admirable for ordinary use, their loveliest praise is to be the blessing of the poor.

Gorgonzola has a sort of hoar prestige, as is confessed by the jokes it has provoked, for all blue cheeses somehow rank in the esteem of commercial travellers above red or yellow; and in England Gorgonzola is always gravely offered for Stilton as a substitute. Probably because of its tendency to become slimy, the odour of Gorgonzola can cling and penetrate with the tenacity of cigar-smoke. Perhaps for this reason, the puritan nose twitches in indignation or expresses itself in music-hall quips which imply that all blue cheeses suffer the same tendency. Short of their final and unpermissible decay, however, this is entirely untrue.

Among green cheeses, English, French, and Italian, Gorgonzola, the most variable and the shortest lived, must take third place.

The second place belongs to ROQUEFORT.

While we know from Homer that Polyphemus kept flocks and ate cheese, the French themselves do not claim more than a Roman origin for Roquefort, which, according to Mr Shand, was 'first mentioned in a chronicle of the Monastery of Conques dating from the year 1070'. It seems to carry us across the Channel and, indeed, to classical times, because the milk from which it is made is not cow's milk but ewe's milk, from the flocks that find pasture upon the slopes of the Cevennes, and because the troglodytic process of its ripening suggests a very ancient origin.

The sheep, by the way, gives milk for only some five months in the year, but on the other hand sheep's milk has twice the amount of cheese-making substance to be found in cow's milk.

The interesting process of its ripening recalls the cave of Polyphemus. In the ninth book of the *Odyssey*, Polyphemus, the Cyclops, made and stored many cheeses from the yield of his ewes and she-goats. Ulysses found the Cyclops's 'cheese-racks loaded with cheeses', some of which, before their owner's return, Ulysses and his companions sacrificed, and others they ate. When Polyphemus returned, he 'sat down and milked his ewes and goats all in due course and . . . then he curdled half the milk [how, is not explained] and set it aside in wicker strainers' (S. Butler's translation).

George Chapman, being an ancient translator, puts it more cheese-wise. He says that Polyphemus

quick did dress
His half milk up for cheese, and in a press
Of wicker press'd it; put in bowls the rest.

The stored cheeses on his shelves presumably must have been pressed for keeping; but the pressing in a wicker basket would suffice to drain the whey and to form a kind of cream-cheese (see page 92).

From the district round Roquefort, in the Department of Aveyron, to which French law limits the famous name, the made cheeses are taken to Roquefort itself in order that they may ripen in the natural limestone caverns. There is virtue in limestone, for soils containing it are deemed the best pasture by dairymen who are cheese-makers. These caverns end in a natural cleft which communicates, like a chimney, with the open air. As this upper air is cooler than that in the caves, presumably from the presence of hot springs in the rock, a current of air, humid and cool, is available in these naturally warm cellars which enables the cheeses to ripen without evaporation and shrinking. So valuable have these natural conditions proved that, when the fame of Roquefort had nursed a great industry for export, vast cellars, often several floors deep, were excavated and tunnels made to the ventilating shaft, to multiply the advantages of the caverns. With Roquefort, in sum, the conditions for ripening are more important than the method of making the curd.

The cheese has a pleasant prickly flavour which should be mellow without being sharp. Its blue veins end in crannies covered with green mould, and this mould, according to the textbooks, is cultivated on bread, which is then crumbled and sprinkled on the curd to produce the fermentation.

The fame of Roquefort has led to many attempts at imitation, not only outside the protected district in France, but in other countries as well. As none of these has, I believe, natural caverns similar to those at Roquefort, attempts have been made to reproduce the same conditions in factories, and also, though the flavour is different, to make this cheese from goat's or cow's milk.

Undoubtedly, the best imitation is the cheese sold under the name of DANISH ROQUEFORT. This is an excellent cheese, but we should respect local names and local products, and no more confuse them in cheese than we do in wine. Even in its class, the semi-hard cheeses, Roquefort is on the soft side. This is why it is covered in tinfoil and is kept by the shops in cold storage. Yet Roquefort claims, with some justification, to attain a uniform quality beyond that of other cheeses. It is best when not too ripe, nor refrigerated.

GEX, though not available here, and indeed not often in France outside the Department of the Ain by the Swiss frontier, may yet be mentioned because the writer remembers it as a blue cheese never to be passed over. Flat and round, the shape of a grindstone, and evenly veined, it is mellower than Gorgonzola, blander than Roquefort, less majestic than Stilton, and a sort of French approach to Wensleydale.

Gex can be had in the neighbourhood of Lyons, and is easily recognisable: a blue cheese, let us remember, for Gex, being the centre and cheese-market of a busy district, gives its name to more than one cheese. Of the other blue cheeses of France I have had no experience, and Roquefort seems to be the only one exported, to England at least. Gex is one of those

French delicacies which are not trumpeted throughout the country but properly prized in a wide region about their home. An example to follow!

Leaving, then, the many blue cheeses of France which must be met in their own districts, we come to the familiar semi-hard and hard cheeses of which Gruyère and Dutch are the best known of the white and red varieties here available.

What is familiarly known as DUTCH cheese is really two varieties: EDAM, the round red croquet-balls, made from fresh but partly skimmed milk, and GOUDA, made from whole milk, and much larger and flatter. Mr Shand evokes a delightful picture of these Dutch cheeses in their own home: 'Few people who have seen pyramids of Têtes de Maures, those crimson-hued cannon-balls, piled on barges and canal quays, are likely to forget the gay note of colour which they add to the doll's-house freshness and trimness of the carefully ordered Dutch scene'.

A more detailed picture of the Toy-land of Holland is given by Mrs Beatrix Jungman in her chapter on DUTCH Cheeses.

Speaking on North Holland and the old city of Edam, she wrote:

'The farms round Edam are large and rich in pasture. The cattle are black and white, and look like the animals out of a Noah's Ark. . . . Almost all the farms are engaged in cheese-making', and 'there are no unpleasant revelations to be made'. The 'whole process is carried through with the most exquisite cleanliness. . . . When the curd is prepared, it is put in moulds, of which the lids are pierced, and left in the cheese-press for fifteen hours. The Dutch farmer, despising all modern inventions, continues to use the ancient cheese-press of his fathers, which is entirely worked by hand. The next process is the salting of the cheese, which takes from ten to fifteen days, according to the size. Then the cheese is well rubbed with melted butter to prevent any cracks in the rind. Lastly, it is washed in vinegar, and then allowed to lie for a month or so to ripen. One morning, after being rubbed with linseed-oil to improve their colour, the cheeses are piled in a boat or on a dog-cart—this is a real dog-cart, that is to say, a cart drawn by dogs—and thus find their way to one of the big markets'.[1]

At Alkmaar, which, thirty years ago, was 'the most important, we followed the golden balls whose transformation from milk into cheese we had watched with so much interest'. The reader will have observed the adjective 'golden' balls, a pretty instance of the way in which eye-witnesses differ in their details, and of the vast mistake of judging the truth of historical testimony by pedantic accuracy, or agreement, in details. Mrs Jungman added that the average weight of these Edam cheeses was 'about four pounds'.[1]

[1] *Holland: Peeps at Many Lands.* A. and C. Black, 1907.

For myself, I do not specially care for its rubber-like elasticity of texture, nor find its pale orange colour and flatness of flavour appealing. Though, here again, the best greatly differs from the average. Edam is the poor but honest member of the cheese-family: highly to be prized as a cheap, nourishing, and sometimes admirable and tasty food—Shand quotes Balzac's tribute that starving genius has been kept alive by it— but apt to become monotonous, and too often flat. This is a personal opinion that it would be dishonest to withhold. Who does not know people who really enjoy it? All foods, from Cornish mackerel to American shaddocks (and, indeed, especially to fruit) taste so much better in the places of their origin that one must be ready and willing to believe that Edam eaten in Holland is more tasty than most of that imported here. To import or to preserve mars Quality.

Gouda, being made from unskimmed milk, is not, however, the more tasty. Can Dutch cheese be admirable for toasting? Mr Shand says so. Yet experience of English cheeses suggests that the richer the cheese the finer when toasted. Hence the pre-eminence of Lancashire on toast.

Edam is made in the north and Gouda in the south of Holland. Both take from two to three months to ripen. The best Edam, to bring out such flavour as is possible to it, needs to be warehoused for six or eight months, for here again cheeses are called ripe when ready for the market, but mature only when they have reached their limit of perfectibility by further storage.

Hard cheeses are usually divided into two classes: those that are smooth and solid in texture, as we know all such cheeses in England; and those dotted with holes or eyes, of which we make none here.

The most familiar is, of course, GRUYÈRE, a hard Swiss cheese, of which the German name is EMMEN-THALER, made from cow's milk. Its famous holes or eyes, which should be the size of hazel-nuts and evenly distributed, are the chief difficulty in making it. They are gas-pockets, and their presence or absence during the process of curing is detected by tapping. For full ripeness Gruyère should be kept in the second of its two curing-rooms for the best part of ten months. Another difference in its making is that no vat is used. The cheese is 'cooked' in a copper vessel called a kettle. Its texture is waxy, with a very shiny surface, especially in the eyes themselves. The flavour is dry and faint, one that invites sipping after each mouthful. It does not survive exposure to the air when cut, and the remnants often offered one in hotels can be very uninviting. Though Gruyère has many admirers, I regard it as an acquired taste. Its varnished surface and waxy texture distinguish it from other cheese. It is held in high esteem by cooks. Brillat-Savarin's *fondu* was made with it.

There is another called true Gruyère, which has no holes but a very few oblong nicks in it. This does not need an acquired taste. It is mellower and less astringent than ordinary Gruyère, and, in my opinion, much nicer. It can be tried at Boulestin's.

Passing now to the semi-hard cheeses, and again beginning with the most familiar, we may start with PORT SALUT. This was first made in the Trappist abbey in Mayenne, from whole or partly skimmed milk. It is a flat, round cheese about one foot in diameter, rather spongy in texture and sometimes with very small holes or eyes. When dry it becomes leathery, and can be so mild as to have almost no flavour at all. In summer, when it is less dry and more creamy, it can have a delicate charm. A 'very subtle cheese', Mr Belloc has called it. It always looks appetising, more appetising than it generally is in England—for anyone at least with an English palate. It is certainly a cheese to be avoided in an indifferent or normal English hotel.

Two cheeses that, gastronomically, belong to the same class as Port Salut are the French PONT L'ÉVÊQUE and the Italian BEL PAESE.

PONT L'ÉVÊQUE comes from Calvados, in Normandy, whence the French cider-spirit or brandy, our apple-jack, takes its name. A small square cheese with a rough thick rind, it has an elastic texture with

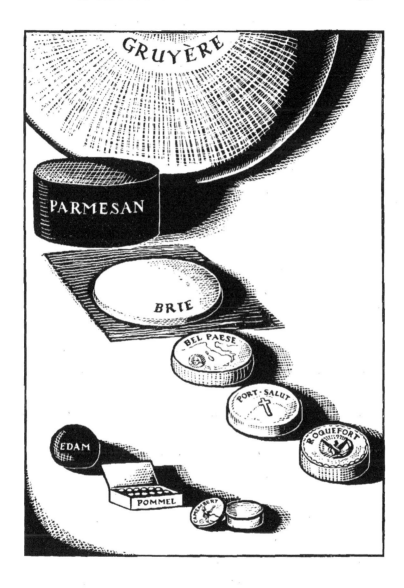

occasional pin-holes reminiscent of Gruyère. This, unlike most technically 'soft' cheese, is not intended to be eaten very fresh. The flavour is not at the vanishing point of the palate, but on the contrary is pleasantly astringent, faintly but agreeably sour. It can be recommended to those who find Port Salut insipid but whose palate inclines to a mild, soft, or rather spongy, cheese.

BEL PAESE, another round, flat, spongy cheese, is also a shade less mild than Port Salut, but still very mild with, however, a cheesy after-taste. If, as some say, it is ousting Port Salut from its former popularity in England, this reserve of flavour may be the explanation. In truth, the question must be asked whether the Port Salut that we are offered over here to-day retains the quality that originally gave it the preference in the market? I would suggest, moreover, that one of the effects of factory-made cheese, already noted in connection with Cheddar, has been to encourage the mild-flavoured cheeses at the expense of the richer and more costly; and that supply has created demand in the topsy-turvy industrial fashion. The larder is following the cellar into oblivion. The storeroom has vanished, and the refrigerator, for all its convenience, is gastronomically a dangerous substitute.

The little, round, felt-like rind of CAMEMBERT needs no description, and to call it the perfection of soft French cheese is definition as well as praise: it leaves the word pluperfect for some other. All we know of its history, and of Madame Harel, its inventor, adds to our appreciation, and the world should join with France in the homage that has led to the unveiling of a statue to her memory.

Camembert originated in 1791 in the commune of that name, which is near Vimoutiers. The making has spread through the region from Caen in the west to Rouen and eastward beyond Paris. It has been, of course, widely imitated, and purchasers should scrutinise the description on the little boxes to be sure of the authentic brand: *Syndicat des Fabricants de Camembert de Normandie;* though, to be sure, cheese of the same name, and often good cheese, is made over a much wider district, not to mention the many inferior made outside France.

None can complain of any want of flavour in a genuine, ripe Camembert cheese. It shows the heights of delicacy to which soft cheeses can aspire. Even the most mild palate cannot be offended by it.

The trouble rather is to find its substance in the right condition: neither hard, which is too early, nor wholly running, which is too late. In England the inevitable tendency is for Camembert to be too hard, since the shops naturally find under-ripe food (or fruit) more convenient than ripeness that cannot last. Since, however, time and (relative) warmth are the conditions needed for ripening, a hard Camembert can be nursed at home if it is wrapped in a damp cloth and kept in a moderately warm temperature, until the whole shall have reached a semi-oozy creaminess.

Contrary to the general opinion, I do not find it essential to peel this difficult cheese on the plate with over-scrupulous care. The flavour of the rind should be negative; it should never be inimical; and, when negative, the smaller scraps are less unpleasing to eat than is the very untidy plate to see when every fragment is detached with difficulty by the finicky. To be perfect, Camembert, like a ripe pear, needs to be eaten, as it were, upon the wing. It waits for no man beyond its brief prime, and it hurries for no hasty shopper. When over-ripe it is unsightly to the eye, distasteful to the nose, unwholesome to the stomach. But, having attained incipient ooziness throughout, not only at its edges, it is beautiful.

This is not a cookery book, but having made with fair success *Camembert au vin blanc,* I can commend it as a delicacy that even the most timid of amateurs does not find difficult. You will find the method at the very end of M. Boulestin's *Simple French Cookery for English Homes,* under the heading 'Crème de Camembert'. Remember, however, that it cannot be prepared off-hand or in a moment, for the peeled cheese requires twelve hours to be steeped in the wine. On the other hand, it is not essential even to the appearance of the dish, a sticky one, that it should be patted into the shape of an enlarged Camembert before serving. Any convenient shape will do; and, as for time, to steep

it the evening before is really no trouble; nor does it
greatly matter—for unprofessional makers—if the dish
is not so dry as it would appear under M. Boulestin's
skilled hand. But a *ripe* Camembert is essential, otherwise the flavour of the cheese itself will be blunted by
the wine and virtually merged in the butter that, after
steeping and drying (the delicate business), is mixed
with it in the proportion of one half. The gust of
Camembert, being of real sovereign flavour, should
not be impaired, but must rule as well as reign over
the other ingredients. To treat it like a limited monarch,
in the English Whig way, is no good.

It would seem impossible to surpass this impeccable
soft cheese, did not BRIE exist to raise the question
of pluperfectness. The very shape of the whole cheese,
a vast thin disk of pale and ochreous gold, set upon
reeds supported by a circular wooden platter, is an
invention in which beauty clearly has been preferred
to vulgar convenience. This is a royal circle, as if the
cheese had instinctively adopted the 'form of perfection' and displayed itself in State, in the manner of a
golden coin, with a diameter out of expectation to its
thinness.

Brie invites hospitality, and so much does appearance
lend to appetite that, when we are forced to buy less
than a half for use at home in the absence of company,
something is missing from the pleasure found in
watching the waiter fetch and cut the whole cheese

E

with due ceremony in a French restaurant. For here, even in restaurants, Brie may be seen in sections only!

Brie is made in the north of France, in the Department of Seine-et-Marne, a little east of Paris; but the name is not protected by law and there are many kinds or qualities, of which the best, made near Meaux, is called Brie de Paris.

Comparison with Camembert, in Meredith's sense,[1] reflects on neither and has some points of interest. For enjoyment at the table, everything true of Camembert is true of Brie, only Brie pushes (as it were) each requirement one degree further. Brie must be creamy, oozing, *coulant,* and throughout. Its colour is nearer that of butter than of cream. It is even more difficult than Camembert to detach from its rind. Its flavour is one degree richer, one degree more lingering and exquisite. Again, it seems to me, the rind of Brie is not merely negative, let alone inimical, but partakes of the very savour of the cheese: so here, too, an undue niceness in paring it seems supererogatory. Do your best, it seems to say, more persuasively than Camembert, but any clinging fragment that you cannot pare will not interfere with my flavour. Moreover, the rind of Brie is less feltlike than Camembert's, softer, thinner, more an extension of the cheese than a different substance surrounding it.

Within it should be a consistent semi-solid, not

[1] 'Observe, I do not compare the wines: I distinguish the qualities.' *The Egoist.*

breaking into two layers when cut. Once cut, if left, it can become horribly dry and uninviting; so, on the whole, a Brie in perfection is a degree more rare, a degree more short-lived, a degree more exceptional than Camembert. Both are 'vintage' cheeses at their ripe moment; and everyone is free to maintain his preference. Neither could be spared. I can only repeat that none would have thought Camembert could be surpassed were it not for Brie. For Brie to be surpassable seems impossible.

It is only at its best, however, for three months in the year, and foreign shops in London often refuse to stock it after April. In fact, December, January, February and March are the best months for soft French cheeses. There is a small delicious form, called Brie *cendré*, caked in ashes, to be had at Boulestin's.

Though not often to be had in England, and, perhaps, not very often beyond the borders of Savoy, REBLOCHONS must be mentioned. It makes a convenient postscript to Brie, for it is a smallish round, flat cheese, very creamy and rich in flavour. So much was it liked that the writer carried one home from Lyons a few years ago. It lives in the memory along with a dish of *fresh* white button-mushrooms served in cream and laced with wine enjoyed during the same visit. Best in the winter, Reblochons was served, to my delight, the other day at Boulestin's.

COULOMMIERS, looking like a rather larger

Camembert, and with a speckled rind, is found both as a ripe and unripe cheese. Compared with Camembert it is a foil only, and I do not remember anyone who has been an enthusiast for it.

GERVAIS, the name of a brand, is a cream-cheese made in Paris, with a rather sour taste. Another, freshly popular in Paris, is FONTAINEBLEAU. In the shape of a little pyramid, it is served with cream poured over it, and can be pleasant in hot weather.

The familiar little POMMEL, that small cylinder wrapped in paper with the ends uncovered, is another of the Petits Suisses, very popular, especially in summer, but needing, of course, to be sprinkled with sugar or salt. The Petits Suisses are not full-cream cheeses. This is a dainty little cheese, attractive to women for this reason, and because it is virtually a sweet, and with the further advantage of providing one helping a cheese, so none is likely to hang over. It has its charm, and also fulfils all the sad requirements of a modern larderless flat, especially in warm weather.

The NEUFCHATEL group has so much in common that the varieties need not be particularised. These 'brands' have their several admirers, and the taste is rather for the type than for one above another among them. They approximate rather to a sweet, but, on the other hand, 'melting without mushiness' on the palate, they offer something distinct from the most mild and flavourless of harder cheeses.

PRIMULA, a Norwegian cheese, obtainable in London in little semicircular boxes, is dead white in colour and soft as the softest paste. It has even less resistance than cream-cheese. It has a pleasant sour flavour, faintly suggestive of anchovy, perhaps because of its salty taste. For this reason it is more like a savoury than a sweet or a cheese, and can also be enjoyed as an unhackneyed form of sandwich. It is, I suppose, a cheese made from whey, for whey cheeses are common in Scandinavia. To eat it regularly might need an acquired taste, but by way of a change, and in small quantity, Primula is worth a trial.

There is also a chocolate-coloured cheese, called NORWEGIAN GOAT'S MILK, the shape of a long, square-sided loaf. Its texture is semi-hard, and its flavour distinct but not pungent. It, too, is worth a trial, and may generally be had at the big grocer's at the corner of Lumley Street, W.1.

There are two other Italian cheeses sometimes listed by the shops, but by no means always available, and both excellent. The first is the semi-hard and blue-flecked DOLCE VERDE. This looks like a flattened roly-poly, is covered in silver paper gaily marked with red and green designs, and is cut in rounds by weight. Its white texture, specked with green, gives to its interior something of the appearance of parsley sauce. It is not easy to describe the flavour: dry, mild but savoury, and of the same sort (though distinct enough)

as Roquefort. Anyone who enjoys a mild blue cheese
will appreciate it. Dolce Verde, I gather, is now
becoming popular, even to the extent of being offered
in the dining-rooms of crowded multiple hotels.

CACCIOCAVALLO, the second cheese, coming
from Naples, is very different. The shape of a vege-
table marrow, its rind has the honey-colour of a
lightly baked loaf. The texture is hard, pale yellow,
dryish and rather crumbly. The pungent bite of its
taste gives to it a flavour rather like that of strong,
sharp Cheddar, of a Cheddar that has an edge to it.
This lingers pleasantly with a prickly after-taste. To the
English palate, for which the cheesiness of cheese is a
virtue, Cacciocavallo is admirable indeed. Both it and
Dolce Verde, and in winter Stracchino—which I have
not tried, but which is said to resemble somewhat
Gex—can be had at 53 Greek Street (Soho Provision
Store). This mention may be useful, for, after several
abortive attempts in the neighbourhood, this was the
first shop at which it was obtainable on demand.
Some people, however, would find Cacciocavallo
too pungent. (We don't.) Its colour is reminiscent of
the Travertine stone which makes much of Rome a
golden honeycomb of buildings.

However obviously incomplete, this selection
typifies the choice of foreign cheeses readily available
here, and it might not be extravagant to add that most
of those omitted would fall naturally into one or other

of the classes that the foregoing examples represent. The foreign range of flavour is wide—from the very pungent to the almost flavourless, from the hardest cheese in the world to creams softer than the softest butter. Most foreign cheeses, at their best, have a sort of *panache*, to set beside the perfect simplicity of the best English, in which last the range is subtly graded from that of the most superlative farm-butter to the apotheosis of all that is meant, in England, by the word Cheese.

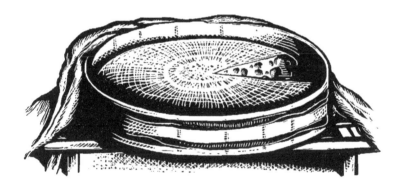

CHAPTER FIVE

THE LITERATURE OF CHEESE

If we discard, as scarcely belonging to the language of appreciation, practical handbooks for dairymen or agricultural students, and old cookery books with their recipes for cheese-making as well as for cheese-dishes, the literature is relieved of two large classes upon its fringe. But, if we then hope for something more than sub-sections or a few pages in general gastronomic works, we shall have to range afield and may return a trifle crestfallen. The English poems and prose in praise of cheese, or in discussion of its qualities, are rather waiting to be collected than readily accessible. Here, the difference between Cheese and Wine, unfortunately, is vast. One is tempted rather to remark how little even famous gastrosophs have contributed: how Brillat-Savarin, belonging to Europe rather than to France, was content with one aphorism; how, like Cobbett himself in *Rural Rides,* our very English classic, Thomas Walker, was silent; how for once Dr C. Louis Leipholdt writes of cheese in its dietetic aspect only; that Mr Morton Shand, though generous, is too brief.

The more reason, be it hoped, that a beginning should be made, and that those with curious learning should fill rather than denounce the gaps in this little survey.

Since English cheese is far older than the fully-formed literature of England, it is convenient to make no beginning before Thomas Tusser, the English Hesiod of the sixteenth century. His famous *Five Hundred Points of Good Husbandry . . . together with The Points of Huswifery,* being a Calendar of rural and domestic Economy for every month in the Year, is a treasury of gnomic verse. It is also a lively record of the agricultural customs and manners of England at the time of the Reformation. Tusser himself, who flourished about 1515 to 1580, and was luckier in his verses than in his farming, was pithily described by Fuller in his *Worthies of Essex* in these words: 'successively a musician, schoolmaster, serving man, husbandman, grazier, poet, more skilful in all than thriving in any vocation. He traded at large in oxen, sheep, *dairies,* grain of all kinds, to no profit. . . . Yet hath he laid down excellent rules'.

The cheese-eater will find them in the section on April's Husbandry, which concludes with 'A Lesson for Dairy-Maid Cisley' in the form of ten faults to avoid in the making of cheese.

Cheese, says Tusser, should not be 'whitish and dry' like Gehazi stricken with leprosy; nor 'too salt' like Lot's wife; nor full of eyes like Argus; nor 'hoven and puffed' like the cheeks of a piper; nor 'leathery' like a cobbler's stuff; nor spotty or 'lazar-like'; nor 'hairy' like Esau; nor full of whey or 'maudlin' like St Mary Magdalen; nor 'scrawling' with mites or gentils; nor 'burnt to the pan' such as a maid, forgetting her curd to run out to watch a passing bishop, may unfairly curse him for having occasioned.

The fourteen couplets and stanzas of this Lesson are Tusser at his homeliest, but room must be found for one or two:

> Leave Lot with her pillar, good Cisley, alone,
> Much saltness in white-meat is ill for the stone.

> If cheese in dairy have Argus's eyes,
> Tell Cisley the fault in her huswifery lies.

> Rough Esau was hairy, from top to the foot,
> If cheese so appeareth, call Cisley a slut.

> As Maudlin wept, so would Cisley be drest,
> For whey in her cheeses not half enough prest.

The little epilogue begins:

> If thou, so oft beaten,
> Amendest by this,
> I will no more threaten,
> I promise thee, Ciss.

On his often charming verse with its Skeltonic lilt
and frequent larklike ripple we must not linger, beyond
remarking that he defined the cheese-making season
to be

> from April beginning till Andrew be past,

that is, until the Saint's day on November 30th. In the
second or Huswifery part of his work, he has a section
on Dinner Matters which should not be overlooked
by our anthologists of Good Cheer.

Tusser may be said to have laid firm foundations.

Shakespeare, who misses nothing wholly, does not
add much, but he has preserved something good in
The Merry Wives, where most of his allusions are to
be found. This is a pregnant reference to Banbury
cheese, which otherwise might be lost to popular
memory. Banbury cheese must have had one thing in
common with Brie, since it was a favourite comparison
for thinness—'like a Banbury cheese, nothing but
paring'.[1] That is the point of Bardolph's exclamation
to Slender in *The Merry Wives:* 'You Banbury cheese!'
Later, in the same play, Shakespeare gives his sanction

[1] From *Jack Drum's Entertainment,* quoted by Steevens.

to the serving of cheese with dessert: a word, covering *both* dishes, that came into use in the seventeenth century.[1] Thus Sir Hugh Evans says to Simple: 'I pray you be gone: I will make an end of my dinner; there's pippins and seese [cheese] to come'. Other allusions in the play suggest a passion for cheese in Welshmen, who have allowed much of their native particular, Caerphilly, to be made outside the Principality.

With the seventeenth century, charming old cookery-books containing directions for making cheese and other dairy lore begin to abound, but, despite their tit-bits, they often belong more to curiosity than to gastronomy. In truth, so long as many, perhaps most, people were accustomed to *make* their own cheeses, it was scarcely necessary to discuss how to *choose* them, or their flavours. The several qualities of cheeses were generally known. We were all good judges then, however much skill in making and degrees of excellence might vary. Uniformity of quality, the blurring

[1] Dessert: 'Skinner, d. 1667, philologist, aged 40, speaks of dessert (fr. Latin *deservire*) as a new word for the "after-course of superfluous delicacies *served* on the removal of the last of the services". It replaced Voider, and the later Issue of the Table. From the opening of the eighteenth century the final course of an English dinner has been called dessert.' *A Book about the Table*, by John Cordy Jeafferson. 2 vols., 1875.

In *The Anatomy of Dessert*, that little classic by E. A. Bunyard (Chatto & Windus, 1933), fruit is the subject with the wines best suited to its varieties. But Thomas Tusser groups together 'cheese, apples and nuts'.

of local differences between neighbour-dairies, was neither expected nor desired. Happy times!

As one example of this homely literature, *The Gentlewoman's Companion*, which Mrs Hannah Woolley printed in 1673, may suffice. Mrs Woolley's section on 'Dayries' gives directions for making cheese and butter.

The 'ever famous' Thomas Muffett, Doctor in Physick, in his *Health's Improvement* or Rules . . . of preparing All sorts of Food, which was 'corrected and enlarged' by Dr Christopher Bennett in 1655, praises Parmesan, Essex cheese, Banbury and Cheshire, 'to which' last pair, he adds, 'the Holland cheeses might be justly compared'. He mentions Parmesan in order to prove that the legendary cheese that sustained Zoroaster for two decades in the wilderness was perfectly credible. In London I have seen a Parmesan that weighed one and a half hundredweight. This would feed a man, who had no other food, for eleven months without stinting. By a simple calculation, Zoroaster's cheese must have weighed one ton, twelve and a half hundredweight, supposing he allowed himself half a pound daily.

In this, the seventeenth, century, we naturally think of the Bible. Though cheese is mentioned enough to show that it was familiar to the ancient Hebrews, and those that Jesse carried at the behest of David to the camp were probably small, or he could hardly have managed ten conveniently, cheese has no place to correspond with that of corn, or bread, or wine. Perhaps the Authorised Version should rather be mentioned as having lent its unwitting sanction to the neglect that, since the Reformation, we are lamenting.

Though Pope's *Satires and Epistles of Horace Imitated* abound in references to fare of all kinds, I do not recall that cheese is celebrated. He speaks somewhere, though, of 'cheese such as men in Suffolk make',[1] and—now that it is too late to save many local cheeses —doubtless people will begin to take an interest in unearthing facts about them. As we have seen, the only named cheese to be celebrated by Shakespeare was Banbury, and it is perhaps of interest to recall that a recipe for making Banbury cheese is contained in the Sloane MS. 1201.

Old recipes, however, can be more tantalising than helpful. As good an instance as any is a recipe for making Stilton, given in *Culina Famulatrix Medicinæ*, written by Ignotus and revised by Dr A. Hunter (3rd edition, 1806). This recipe, in less than fifty

[1] The hardness of Suffolk cheese can be guessed from the saying: 'Hunger will break through stone walls and anything except a Suffolk cheese.' A modern writer even exclaims: 'Suffolk, long infamous for its hard, horny, flet-milk cheeses, which Swift called "cartwheels", and farm-labourers designate "bang".' *A Book about the Table*, by John Cordy Jeafferson, Vol. II, p .261.

words, defeats its end. Only the appended Observation that 'Stilton cheeses are seldom used till two years old' gives any glimpse of the complicated processes. A recipe for cream-cheese, on a later page, is considerably longer! His reiterated counsel, that the rennet be 'sweet', suggests only one essential out of many.

In his *Polite Conversation* Swift refers to Oxfordshire cheese. In this dialogue Lord Smart mentions 'an odd kind of fellow' who, 'when the cheese came upon the table, pretended to faint; so somebody said, Pray, take away the cheese; No, said I; pray, take away the fool: Said I well?'. To this Colonel Atwit rejoins: 'Faith, my lord, you served the coxcomb right enough; and therefore I wish we had a bit of your lordship's Oxfordshire cheese'. A whole one is brought immediately, and Miss Notable is teased for refusing to cut it. In the same dialogue the old notion that cheese digests everything except itself—to which my mother used to add 'and bread digests cheese'—is introduced, no doubt as an indispensable commonplace. This saw, known in very many forms, perhaps explains, or arose to justify, the custom of serving cheese at the end of a meal of which it is not the staple. Its metrical forms do not improve the adage, but we find the same precept in mediaeval Latin: *caseus est nequam quia concoquit omnia secum.*

Cheese-mites, the terror of vegetarians, have given a neat little poem to us, beginning:

The cheese-mites asked how the cheese got there,
And warmly debated the matter;
The orthodox said it came from the air,
And the Heretics said from the platter.[1]

In the middle of the eighteenth century, the pride of the Cheshire folk in their cheese was expressed in *A Cheshire Cheese Song,* which was popular enough to be set to music, and was eventually published in London in 1786 with a drawing by Rowlandson on its title-page. The composer, appropriately, was a Welshman, Edward Jones. Of its three, apparently anonymous, verses, the following (first and second) are the best:

A CHESHIRE CHEESE SONG

A Cheshireman sail'd into Spain
To trade for merchandize;
When he arrived from the main,
A Spaniard him espies.
Who said, You English rogue, look here!
What fruits and spices fine
Our land produces twice a year.
Thou hast not such in thine.

The Cheshireman ran to his hold
And fetch'd a Cheshire cheese,
And said, Look here, you dog, behold!
We have such fruits as these.

[1] *Notes and Queries,* Twelfth Series (Index).

> Your fruits are ripe but twice a year,
>   As you yourself do say,
> But such as I present you here
>   Our land brings twice a day.

Rowlandson's drawing shows the Cheshireman knocking down the Spaniard, as related in the third verse.[1] A good Cheshire saying—*Cheat and the cheese will show*—should encourage us to-day to learn how to choose a cheese, for milk over-skimmed, and a cow fed either not on grass or on oil-cake, will betray itself in texture, sometimes disagreeably in taste, to the wary. Spring Stiltons are made from cows' milk that is the product of poor pasture or artificial food. When the summer grass chances to be poor, the autumnal Stiltons will not ripen by November, and appear, if disposed of and placed on sale, in the New Year after careful nursing. Such cheeses cannot be of the finest quality.

This Cheshire cheese song also reminds us that cheese had become sufficiently honoured to be celebrated in various ways, and that its making was ushered in or concluded with rural festivities. As Tusser has recorded, the cheese-making season began in April. Consequently, it was natural that it should form part of the junketings on May Day. 'In Gloucestershire', wrote Mr F. W. Hackwood, 'this festive day was once utilised to honour the production of its

---

[1] The full text is given in *Notes and Queries*, Twelfth Series, Vol. IX, p. 254.

F

native dairies, the famous Gloucester cheese. At Randwick, near Stroud, the custom was to carry in procession to the church three cheeses decked with flowers, on three litters, to the accompaniment of shout, song, and music. They were divested of their decorations and rolled three times round the church. They were then rehabilitated, carried back to the village in the same state, and finally cut up for distribution among the inhabitants.'[1] Such customs endure in the still civilized corners of Europe, for a friend tells me of 'the cheese that the Basque shepherds bring to Poitou in the spring to the sound of pipes'.

In the eighteenth century, moreover, the cheese-maker was recognized officially. He could aspire to the public appointment of Cheesemonger to the Government, which, under the narrow landed aristo-cracy that then ruled the kingdom, was perhaps more gratifying than the wider favour that made many tradesmen 'purveyors' to the Hanoverian monarchs. Woodforde mentions the former post in his *Diaries*. He also has a few details about cheeses. He mentions Cottenham cheese, and speaks of a 'cheese-spitter with an ivory handle' that he bought at Norwich in 1790 for 2s. 6d. Presumably, he meant a trier. He also alludes to 'ramakins', an anglicised form of the French *ramequin*: the familiar term in French cookery for a dish of toasted cheese and bread, sometimes in the

[1] *Good Cheer*, by Frederick W. Hackwood. 1911. See Hone's *Table Book*, under April 1827.

form of 'small slices of breadcrum covered with a farce made of pounded cheese, eggs and other ingredients baked in a pie-pan'. This dish was popular as far back as Queen Anne's reign, and it continued to be so far into the nineteenth century, as we know from the admirable Kirwan's *Host and Guest* (1864). 'At large dinners in London cheese is oftenest eaten in the form of ramequins, or grated Parmesan, and other preparations.' But ramekin, as the word has since become, is carrying us forward too quickly.

At the beginning of the nineteenth century, Tom Moore, the poet, had some claims to our attention, for the widely read Jeafferson remarked in 1875, that 'With the exception of Leigh Hunt and Tom Moore, England has not produced during the last hundred years a single author, chiefly famous for his poetry, who may be named among eminent epicures'.[1] This virtually forgets Sydney Smith with his humorous poem on salad; his letter about grouse when shot by a Scotch metaphysician; his enjoyment of the sauces of Dives and his treatment of the sores of Lazarus; his rhymed reply to an invitation to dine with the Fishmongers' Company, beginning

> Much do I love, at civic treat,
> The monsters of the deep to eat—

a serious omission, for Jeafferson does not (or could not) repair it when he turns to prosemen of the same

[1] *A Book about the Table,* by J. C. Jeafferson. Vol. II, p. 278.

century. Noting, moreover, that Jeafferson gives no example of Tom Moore's gastrosophy, and that a more famous epicure, Peacock, severely reviewed Moore's novel, *The Epicurean*, our curiosity weakens; and the amiable but erratic Hunt scarcely re-awakens it. If my memory serves, neither Peacock himself nor Meredith contributed anything remarkable on Cheese; and this lament only diminishes when we arrive at contemporary and almost contemporary literature.

We may fill the interval by a glance at one or two of the cookery-books for which the nineteenth century was famous.

The old ones, from the sixteenth century onward, are surveyed in Jeafferson's own chapter on the subject at the conclusion of his widely ranging work. Here I would only mention the later examples that I have found of use on the literature of cheese. One reason for this brevity is that it took a long time before Cookery was separated from Medicine[1] in the minds of English writers. Since then, we have gone to the other extreme and must deplore the attention wasted on the very obscure pseudo-science of dietetics, about which we know so little, and the correspondingly recent neglect of the art of dining—for invalids also the true 'handmaid of health'—on which we have inherited so much. These cookery books developed

[1] 'For two thousand years and upwards food and physick were one and the same thing.' *The Compleat Housewife or Accomplished Gentlewoman's Companion*, by E. Smith. 1736.

into 'companions' for ladies living in the country. Consequently the making of cheese, and recipes for different kinds, have a prominent place in the best of them.

After the famous Mrs Glass(e)'s *Art of Cookery made Plain and Easy*, 1745, with its tiny section on how to choose cheeses, its recipe for 'potted Cheshire cheese' that a friend well qualified to speak tells me is 'delicious', we are fairly launched on such cheese-literature as these cookery books provide.

Mrs Glasse (or Glass, for the name is spelt both ways, and her book, like its kind, appeared anonymously) was superseded in fashion by Mrs M. E. Rundell or Rundle, of Devonshire, who, also under the modest anonymity of 'a Lady', published in London in 1819 her famous *New System of Domestic Cookery*.[1] This, in its comprehensiveness, is a literary forerunner of Mrs Isabella Beeton, but in a more discursive and confiding form. What is there that Mrs Rundell does not touch on, what advice does she omit? She details at some length the ways of making and preserving cheese—there was a cheese-room in most contemporary houses—and gives a recipe for Sage cheese that has been recommended to me by a lady who has tried it successfully. The flavour of her style, slightly sententious and mildly admonitory, has, moreover, the pleasure of its period. From these books one begins to realise the

[1] It was published previously at Exeter. The edition named above may not have been John Murray's first edition.

amount of labour involved when there were no such things to be bought as bleached almonds, when rennet had to be prepared at home from the body of a calf, when the housekeeper had nothing to begin with except raw materials in their most primitive, sometimes still living, state. Thus an earlier writer, E. Smith, in her *Compleat Housewife,* which had reached its twelfth edition by 1744, gives directions for making rennet, besides four sorts of cream-cheese. She has a recipe for 'a slipcoat cheese', for ordinary Cheddar, and for 'a new market cheese to cut at 2 years old'. The 'Queen's cheese' is also mentioned. For such literature the reader is referred to *Old Cookery Books and Ancient Cuisine,* by W. Carew Hazlitt.

On several other books of the same type, usually directed to the young wife and often offered to one who had had no previous experience of living in the country, I must not linger. They have their interest and their pathos. They evoke the domestic background on a level more substantial than even Jane Austen touched. We lose the daily circumstance of country life in their period without them. We conceive a new interest, verging on admiration, for the Victorian wives whose guides they were; and their households, if strenuous, seem richer in humane virtue and in dignity than is possible to the mistress of any flat.

But one word must be said on the book that succeeded Mrs Rundle's, for it should have a place in the history of authorship, if not of cheese. This was Miss

Eliza Acton's *Modern Cookery in all its Branches,* published in 1845. After the failure of her poems, and some years spent as a governess, Miss Acton called on Mr Longman and astonished him by saying that, wishing to write some book that was really needed, if he would give her a subject she would write it for him. He suggested a good cookery-book, but refused to 'advise her' to write, saying circumspectly that only if he were sure of her ability would he do so. Miss Acton had no particular qualifications for such a task. However, after nine years' work, and a correspondence that drew every friend, epicure and chef into its persuasive embrace, she at last produced her volume. The story has a charming moral for all authors. Her patient determination was rewarded. The book proved so successful that she was provided for till the end of her life.

From this excursion into the byways of cheese-literature it is pleasant to turn to an *Ode to Cheese* which, if not originally written in English or by an Englishman, has been translated into decent English verse. This is Jethro Bithell's rendering of the poem by M. Thomas Braun.

As much as we have room for is the following:

ODE TO CHEESE

God of the country, bless today Thy cheese,
For which we give Thee thanks on bended knees.
Let them be fat or light, with onions blent,

Shallots, brine, pepper, honey; whether scent
Of sheep or fields is in them, in the yard
Let them, good Lord, at dawn be beaten hard.
And let their edges take on silvery shades
Under the moist red hands of dairymaids;
And, round and greenish, let them go to town
Weighing the shepherd's folding mantle down;
Whether from Parma or from Jura heights,
Kneaded by august hands of Carmelites,
Stamped with the mitre of a proud abbess,
Flowered with the perfumes of the grass of Bresse,
From hollow Holland, from the Vosges, from Brie,
From Roquefort, Gorgonzola, Italy!
Bless them, good Lord! Bless Stilton's royal fare,
Red Cheshire, and the tearful, cream Gruyère.

The phrase 'stamped with the mitre' is interesting. Such stamping was not peculiar to monastic cheeses, for Parson Woodforde, in his Diary for 1799, records the arrival of a big cheese from Somerset bearing the King's Arms embossed upon its side. Perhaps it was supplied by the Cheesemonger to the Government.

Charles Lamb's appreciation glows refreshingly in a letter to Thomas Allsop (1823) thanking him for the gift of a Stilton: 'Your cheese is the best I ever tasted. Mary . . . has sense enough to value the present; for she is very fond of Stilton. Yours is the delicatest, rainbow-hued, melting piece I ever flavoured'.

Later Victorian literature maintained the wholesome

current of cookery and table-books, but only a few pages in them belong to the literature of cheese, and fewer still perhaps to the literature of its appreciation. In the first edition of Mrs Beeton's *Household Management* (1861) there are, however, some useful remarks upon Cheese, and a recipe for making Stilton, 'or British Parmesan as it is sometimes called'! Mrs Beeton must be taken to represent in her epoch the extensive literature that she herself crowned.

Of the more gossipy books that succeeded, the choice is embarrassing so numerous are they; but Mrs Pennell's *Guide for the Greedy,* first published in 1896 under the title of *The Feasts of Autolycus,* with its chapter on 'Indispensable Cheese', is typical, though coming, strictly, from America. She says frankly: 'Preposterous it would be truly to serve the mild-flavoured plebeian species from Canada or America after a carefully ordered dinner'. For its conclusion she recommends 'Port Salut, with its soothing suggestion of monastic peace' and as 'a safeguard against indigestion'.

There seemed to be a lull in this literature just before the War, but, if so, it has been abundantly redeemed afterward. The feverish 'twenties produced a spate of table-books, and the subject fully recovered its native dignity when George Saintsbury in 1920 issued his famous little work on Wine. Having yet to discover a similarly scholarly book on Cheese, we must be grateful for Hilaire Belloc's essay,[1] in which a great man, for all his brevity, lifts the subject to its right level in human history and among humane interests.

Listen to this:

'If antiquity be the only test of nobility, then cheese is a very noble thing. . . . The lineage of cheese is demonstrably beyond all record.'

Again: 'Cheese does most gloriously reflect the multitudinous effect of earthly things, which could not be multitudinous did they not proceed from one mind. . . . You can quote six cheeses perhaps which the public power of Christendom has founded outside the limits of its ancient Empire—but not more than six. I will quote you 253 between the Ebro and the Grampians, between Brindisi and the Irish Channel.

'I do not write vainly. It is a profound thing.'

We can search far and find nothing better. This strikes the note for which we have been looking. With the same author's magnificent 'Heroic Poem in Praise of Wine', it entitles Mr Belloc to a high place in the literature also of gastronomy. To end with it would be seemly, were not someone sure to complain that Mr Chesterton's famous line had been omitted:

Stilton, thou shouldst be living at this hour!

To this parody there is a worthy fellow: Mr J. B. Morton's 'Poem to a Shropshire Lad'.

[1] *First and Last:* essay ' On Cheeses'. Methuen, 1911.

It begins:

Loveliest of cheese, the Cheddar now. . . .

and rare indeed is he who can quote the rest of it! But
I forbear.

In *The Flying Inn* Mr Chesterton made a great
cheese one of the principal characters. It rolls along
the story.

Now, though this bird's eye view of the subject
could be enlarged by hundreds of parallel references,
practical or curious, does it not incline us to admit
that, with the Belloc essay for measurement, the fine
literature of cheese has yet to be written? It need not
be extensive, but it should be very good.

In the words of Jeafferson, 'epicures of the highest
order are always persons of considerable intellect'.

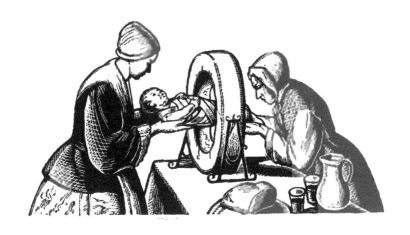

CHAPTER SIX

REMARKS AND CURIOSITIES

GROANING CHEESE

This was a large cheese, so called from its being in old
days supplied by the husband against the time of his
wife's delivery. At the birth of the child it was cut in
the centre in such a way that by degrees a ring was
formed, through which the child was ceremonially
passed on the day of his Christening. The custom is
described by John Brand in his *Observations on Popular
Antiquities,* Vol. II, edited by Sir H. Ellis, 1841.

'FILLED CHEESE'

The name of a practice that should be illegal, by which
a large proportion of animal fats or margarine is
added, in pretence of whole milk, to skimmed. Any

delicate cheeses thus adulterated lose their quality, and the unfortunate eater possibly his health.

VEGETABLE CHEESE

A so-called 'cheese' is made from the Soya bean, which has many uses, but the one thing it does not produce is milk-curd.

SAGE CHEESE AND PINEAPPLE CHEESE

Not to be confused with the foregoing, Sage Cheese (and similar flavouring) was once common in England, and still is in America. It means the addition of a flavouring by an infusion of sage. It gives a greenish hue and a characteristic taste.

The term Pineapple cheese refers, I believe, to the shape, and is now common only in America.

D'ISIGNY

This is not the name of any French cheese, though the place is known for its butter. The so-called d'Isigny cheeses, often attached to famous names, are American varieties, in which the addition of sacred names like Brie refers to the size.

EARLY DATES OF ENGLISH VARIETIES

Professor Thorold Rogers, in his *History of Agriculture and Prices,* gives the following:

Essex and Gloucester, 1594; Cheshire and Suffolk, 1655; Cream, 1686; Stilton, 1771; Double Gloucester, 1772.

In the *Calendar of State Papers,* Domestic Series, is a letter written in the 1630's by Viscount Conway to Lord Poulett about Cheddar cheeses—'Now they are grown to be in such esteem at Court that they are bespoken before they are made'.

Gervase Markham (?1568-1637), in *The English House Wife,* mentions four varieties: New Milk or Morning's milk, the best ordinarily made; Nettle Cheese, 'the finest summer cheese'; Flitten-milk, the 'coursest' (*sic*), and Eddish cheese or Winster cheese, apparently indistinguishable from summer cheese. See *Notes and Queries,* Twelfth Series, Vol. VIII.

THE AGE OF CHEESES

Near Zermatt, 'the rank of a family is determined by the age and quality of the cheese in its larder'. There are patricians who own cheeses a century old. These are served only on solemn occasions: 'Christenings, weddings, or funerals'. In 1910 it was reported that an ancient cheese dating from 1785 had been discovered in a concealed shelter at Les Ormonts. It was as hard as a rock and had to be cut with a saw. It is reported to have tasted good. See Walsh: *Handbook of Curious Information,* Lippincott, Philadelphia, 1913.

CHEESE AUCTIONS

At High Bridge, in Somerset, frequent auction-sales of cheese have long been held; and a considerable trade with Wales is maintained from thence, particularly by the making of Caerphilly.

THOMAS HARDY'S PREFERENCE

Blue Vinny, which not everybody likes, was a cheese enjoyed by Thomas Hardy. It is always to be had in Dorchester, but not easily anywhere else.

CHEESE AND TOBACCO

Only monsters smoke at meals, but a monster assures me that Gorgonzola best survives this malpractice. Clearly, some pungency is necessary, and confidence suggests rather Cacciocavallo—which could 'survive anything' (the monster said).

HOLES IN CHEESE

A holeless Gruyère or Emmenthal is sometimes called 'blind', and one with many pin-holes a 'niszler'.

THE 'GENIUS LOCI'

His existence in old dairies seemed to be proved when transported dairymaids, chosen for their skill, failed to repeat their successes in a distant country. When the pasture, the breed of cows, the care in making, could not explain the failure, the *genius loci* was supposed by the materialists to be a Deposit of Bacteria which, in the course of generations, had made the original *cella lactaria* or dairy the fittest breeding-ground for them, and therefore the spot best able to produce a particular flavour. Though research can analyse neither wine nor poetry, it refuses to admit any presence not imprisonable in its test-tubes and retorts. Let us, having the original cheeses, continue to rejoice in the Mysteries that bewilder laboratories.

'Food Value'

While the enumeration of calories is a very untrustworthy guide to the nutriment obtainable from foods, it is said that a quarter of a pound of cheese is the nutritive equivalent of ten eggs or of three-quarters of a pound of rump steak. What don't they say?

A Farmers' Wrinkle

Many farmers assert that, even from the same cow, evening's milk is richer than morning's. Hence, in part, the frequent blending of the two. Before the use of 'starters' was not the exception, milk twelve hours old, of course, was valuable for the acidity it was gaining, and such natural acidity was the only 'starter' anciently used.

Green Cheese

In the cookery-books of the seventeenth, and even of the eighteenth centuries, a cheese was called 'green' from its newness, not from its colour, and the adjective meant that the whey had been only half pressed out. Even Kirwan, writing in 1864, in his chapter on 'Cheese and Salads' in *Host and Guest,* seems to have preferred Stilton in its white state. Though he remarks that 'Epicures prefer a Stilton cheese with a green mould', he adds 'but the best . . . are . . . without any appearance of mouldiness'. Throughout, he is an advocate of mild cheese.

MRS BEETON SAYS:

Though it would be a crime to omit this famous authoress, in her *Household Management* (*e.p.* 1861) she does not enlarge. Her General Observations are sensible: her particular include these: that in Holland it is the practice to coagulate the milk with muriatic acid instead of rennet; that in Thuringia and Saxony cheese is made from milk and potatoes. Mrs Beeton's oracular pronouncement on Cream-cheese has been given on page 29.

A DEFINITION OF SLIPCOAT

Simmonds's *Trade Dictionary* (1858) gives the following: 'Slip-coat, new made cheese; a small and very rich variety of Yorkshire cheese, not unlike butter, but white'. This bears out the remarks made upon York cheese (p. 29 *seq*). Slipcoat was, in fact, an early synonym for cream-cheese. The latest printed use of the term that I have met was in 1911. One of the earliest, 1669, refers to 'excellent slipp-coat cheese' made of 'good morning milk, putting cream to it'. Therefore Slipcoat was not a full cream, nor yet a full milk, cheese. YORK is made from fresh, rich milk.

G

Yoghurt or Yoghout

This is not a cheese, but a sour, fermented liquor made from milk in the Levant and in Turkey. Thus, strictly, the dictionaries. But the writer of the following Letter adds, privately, 'I *eat* it: quite a lot. But, here at any rate, it looks like Junket. I eat it with jam, salt, or nothing at all.' Youghourt (the name has many spellings) is sold in London by the Blue Pot, 48 Archer Street, W.11. I, too, have eaten Yaghourt Cream-cheese: very white, mildly sour, very agreeable.

Also the dead white, firmer Fetta, a Bulgarian cheese, hardish, sourish, but good. Fetta, argue how you may, goes well with butter on bread. The butter is a cushion, and takes the edge off for the shyer palate.

Try them!

If You Please

The critical reader is invited to remember that Cheese-makers, Vendors, and Authors of text-books often contradict one another on 'matters of fact', such as the kind (or kinds) of milk used in the making of Roquefort, the reason for calling some Gloucester Single and some Double, etc.

Being no dairyman, the present writer, therefore, has frequently had to choose between conflicting assertions. It would be rash to assume that such facts are agreed in the sense that their recorders are unanimous. In a dairy error would be serious. In the dining-room it should not mar either good eating or good talk.

Friendship 'sends some precious instance of itself'.—W. S.

A LETTER FROM ITALY

An old friend of the writer who has long made her home in Italy has sent the following delightful Letter with permission for its inclusion:

'Arriving at Sparanise, on the main line to Naples, the best thing was to wait in a hay-field, listening to the larks pass the time before a branch line jogged you into Formia—the death-place of Cicero—half-way between Gaeta and Naples: a straggling town with a hundred streams rushing down to the sea from the hills behind it. These make it very clean. Otherwise you took a carriage from Terracina, the old gate of the Kingdom of Naples, and passed through Itri, where the horse usually broke down. If it did, you had time to look at the Castle, but you didn't. You found instead a twelfth-century stone house with the ground-room open to the street.

'Itri is in the country of olives: in the room there was an olive-press and you saw the stones of the olives being crushed out of them by the revolving stone. The stone was attached to a stout rope, and this to a donkey who went slowly round and round. The smell

of the oil is everywhere. You slip on oil in the streets. . .
But after a few days you discover what is the real
product of the place. It is Cheese.

'In the main square there is the shop of La Mozzarellara, facing the sea. The Mozzarellara is the ancient
dame who sells the MOZZARELLA, a snow-white
cheese of Buffalo milk, neither hard nor soft. The little
shop is full of this. Some of it is fashioned into the
shapes of animals and "rude" images of Saints. La
Mozzarellara looks like a Chelsea jug: very squat and
square, with ten chins under a black straw-hat, an
impassive face, and ear-rings which seem to drag the
lobes of her ears to where might have once been her
waist.

'At every corner they sell RICOTTA, fresh from
the mountains: a white, hard-curd cheese pressed into
crinkly baskets which make a pattern on it. This is
made from ewes' milk curdled at dawn in the rocks
of the hills.[1] There must be about five kinds. At midday donkeys pass with panniers. On the panniers are
wide trays filled with what look like white *éclairs*
dipped in green caraway seeds. Instead, they are com-
pact little soft cheeses, rather dry than wet and with
a taste of spicy grass in them. The caraway seeds are
little seedling herbs, a cross between rosemary and

[1]If this be compared with the description in the *Odyssey* of
the cheeses made by Polyphemus (see *ante*, p. 45), it would appear
that the Cyclops made and ate Ricotta cheese.—O. B.

thyme. They were most appetising spread on crusty bread. I don't remember their name or that of their milcher.

'Then there is the horse's cheese, CACCIOCAVALLO (made of mare's milk), very large and smoky, so I suppose it is smoked. Then there is the common PECORINO goat's cheese which the Italian peasant uses in lieu of the cheese of Parma to grate on his soup. It is very strong and biting.

'Then there are the PROVATURE, whether sheep or Buffalo I forget, and the SCAMORZA. You learn, as you see the goats passing through Formia, that most of all these cheeses come from the rich pastures round Minturno, one of the last villages before you reach the plain of Naples.

'The MASCARPONE is a large ball-shaped kind of Petit Suisse tied up in muslin—a little kerchief for each. At home, in town, these can be spread on a chocolate-cake to make a sweet, or be eaten with strawberries. In the country you eat them with bread and salt: so you see their flavour is amphibious. (I don't like them much, and think it is possible they can also be made from the cow, for there is a kind of them in Milan.) They are a sort of Devonshire clot, without the clot: what in nursery days was called "too rich". There are no amenities on this stretch of the Appian Way: no butter but what arrives half-tired from Milan, but I remember that two of the *éclair* cheeses and an egg and fruit was quite an attractive luncheon on the way to Minturno, for about three weeks. At the restaurant in Formia (for supper) you chose soup and an omelette, as the oil for cooking the fish was the oil of Itri, not of Lucca. And what was there to put in either? Just cheese.

'The Cheese of a life-time:

'On the plateau over Orvieto on a day in May—the air so clear, so still, so scentless except for the hay and flowers that a host of white butterflies smelt even that *new-born* cheese and fluttered around—we had arrived after 5 miles' walk, the way slowly winding up and up through chestnut-groves and corn-fields: on the top an empty farmhouse, an orchard, mulberry trees. It was of course my fault that we had brought nothing to eat. I went into the house—it was full of silkworms on trays, rustling and eating. Out in the orchard, however, my companion, I don't remember how, had provided the miracle: a flask of wine, a loaf of bread, and a slab of fresh PECORINO cheese (there wasn't any "thou" for either, as both had come up there to escape from Analysis which accompanied "thou" in his flat). But that cheese was Paradise; and the flask was emptied, and a wood-dove cooing made you think that the flask's contents were in a crystal goblet instead of an enamel cup—one only—and the cheese broken with the fingers—a cheese of cheeses.

'Cheese, I think, was never given to us at school in

England. I can't think why, as it is cheap. Cheese is one of *my* chief columns of nutrition. It contains Phosphates and Lime! It goes on anything and everywhere in this house: the soup, the spaghetti, the eggs, the spinach. (This is Parmesan.) When of the proper quality, it can be cut with a good knife into almost veils, 2 inches square. This, eaten with toast, finishes many a non-hungry meal. It solaces a non-salt diet to those who suffer absence of salt. It can be introduced into fish-pie and meat roll. It is invaluable in a spinach soufflé. In an actual soufflé it mixes well with the requisite amount of Gruyère. It is a good friend and never becomes propinquitous (the word is added for you!). Cheese, being, like literature, the right word in the right place, is awful in the wrong, to wit—in railway-carriages eaten "strong" by hungry people; by temperamental Slavs at 5 in the afternoon; by lady-friends who—expecting late visitors—ring for a hunk from the kitchen and eat it (such is the appetite of health) on a velvet sofa sans plate, sans serviette—which reminds me of the cheese you pinched from mouse-traps to put in the doll's-house—What cheese was *that?* And the cheese you smell in the city of Lyons, which is everywhere—it is only to be compared with the smell of the confessional boxes in old basiliche. I've never met it actually.

'My favourite cheese, if I ask myself sincerely, a good (no preservatives) stiff whipped *raw cream*—

nearer than not to the turn—kept on ice for some hours and then mixed with pistacchio nuts. Eaten with Pineapple. Goodbye!

GILLIAN F.

'P.S. Reader, cheese eaten with the sounds of the cicala—the midday heat—the tiredness of the climb— or enhanced only by the cool and pristine wine—No, only a little hunger would be enough for it and— perhaps—youth in the soul. Search for it, try it, and return in the cool of the day. You will see the Duomo again flame from the approaching town and hear the bells grow nearer; but you will be returning with light feet or dancing because now stayed and fortified —even for the cold eyes of Luca Signorelli—even for the judgment of the DAMNED.'

G.

A LITTLE BIBLIOGRAPHY

(Books other than those mentioned in the text)

The Book of Cheese. By Charles Thom and Walter W. Fisk. Macmillan, 1925. (A comprehensive American work on cheese-making in all its branches, with particular reference to factory-practice.)

Cheese-making. Ministry of Agriculture and Fisheries. Bulletin No. 43. (Very useful.)

Cheshire: Its Cheese-makers. By E. Driver. Casaubon Derwent. Bradford, 1909.

Milk, Cheese and Butter. By J. Oliver. 362 pp. London, 1894.

Of Cottage and Cream Cheeses. By Florence Daniel. 32 pp. C. W. Daniel, 1927.

Lancashire Cheese-making. By R. Richardson. 32 pp. Preston, 1921.

Les Fromages. By M. Des Ombiaux. 1926. (Useful.)

The Compleat Housewife. By E. Smith. 1744. (12th edition.) (This contains, among others, a recipe for making Slipcoat cheese.)

The Pleasures of the Table: an Account of Gastronomy from

Ancient Days to Present Times. By George H. Ellwanger, 1909. (A discursive American book. Useful bibliography.)

The Art of Dining. By Abraham Hayward. (Worth reading.)

Host and Guest. By A. V. Kirwan. London, 1864. (A book to own.)

Common-Sense Dietetics. By C. Louis Leipholdt, F.R.C.S., London, 1911. (*o.p.,* but long overdue for reprinting.)

The Banquet: in Three Cantos. 1819.

The Last Remedy

Where fish is scant and fruit of trees,
Supply that want with butter and cheese.

THOMAS TUSSER

Lightning Source UK Ltd.
Milton Keynes UK
UKHW010152310821
389756UK00001B/80